935

04. JUN

26. JUN

14. AUG 07

28. MAR

27. JUN 08

01. SEP 08

18. MAR 08

16. DEC 08

D0571286

1001 little
housekeeping miracles

Fleur Barrington

CARLTON
BOOKS

THIS IS A CARLTON BOOK

Text and design copyright © 2007
Carlton Books Limited
Illustrations copyright © Carol Morley

This edition published by
Carlton Books Limited 2007
20 Mortimer Street
London W1T 3JW

ISBN-10: 1-84442-096-5

ISBN-13: 978-1-84442-096-4

Printed and bound in Dubai

Executive Editor: Lisa Dyer
Senior Art Editor: Zoë Dissell
Design: Ed Pickford
Copy Editor: Gillian Holmes
Illustrator: Carol Morley
Production: Caroline Alberti

This book reports information and opinions which may be
of general interest to the reader. Neither the author nor the
publisher can accept responsibility for any accident, injury
or damage that results from using the ideas, information or
advice offered in this book.

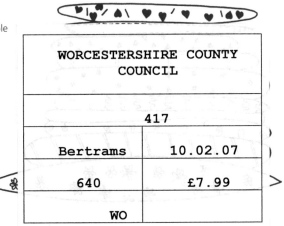

INTRODUCTION

Did you know that lemons, bicarbonate of soda and white vinegar are domestic lifesavers or that you can treat scratches on wood with a halved Brazil nut?

Within these pages you'll find 1001 little housekeeping miracles gathered together from all kinds of experts to help you turn your house into a real home. Take a room-by-room tour or dip in to discover just how to organize your laundry or handle any household emergency. From glassware that gleams to editing wardrobes and from silver that sparkles to caring for wood finishes, you'll find everything you need to run a happy, healthy and cleaner home. Let little and often be your maxim – efficient housekeeping leaves you more time to enjoy life.

Top ten little housekeeping miracles

42
KEEP BISCUITS FRESH FOR LONGER
(see Smart Cookie, page 16)

96
DEODORIZE YOUR WASTE DISPOSAL
(see A Touch of Zest, page 28)

114
REMOVE CUTLERY STAINS
(see Family Silver, page 33)

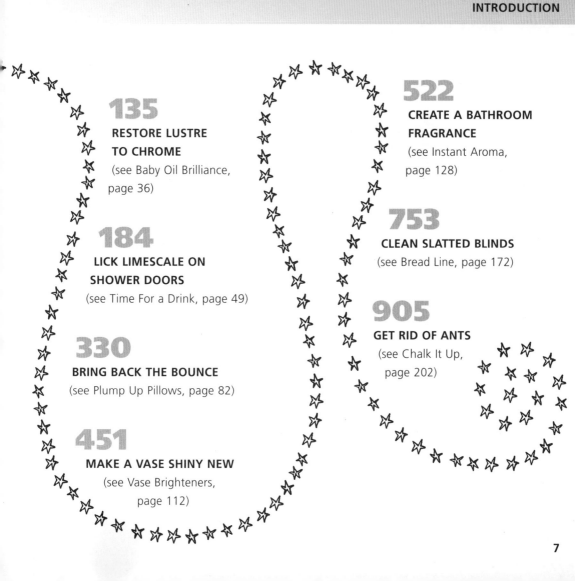

THE KITCHEN

dishwashing

1 CRYSTAL CLEAR

To brighten cloudy crystal, submerge one glass in a bowl of vinegar for 10 minutes. Rinse, dry and hold up to the light. If there is no improvement, a chemical reaction has taken place causing the glasses to become 'etched' and there is nothing you can do. But if it looks better, submerge all the glasses in warm white vinegar for 1–2 hours. Wipe with a soft, lint-free cloth. Treat any remaining cloudiness with fine-grade steel wool dipped in vinegar.

2 DISHWASHER DETERGENT

Mix 250 ml (8 ½ fl oz) borax with 125 ml (4 ¼ fl oz) baking soda for a phosphate-free automatic dishwashing product.

3 SQUEAKY CLEAN

If your washing-up liquid detergent produces too many bubbles, add just a few drops to comfortably hot water. Wipe first to remove dirt and food from dishes. If a plate is really clean, it will squeak as you run a finger across it.

4 A PERFECT FINISH

Clip a finish protector (available from supermarkets) to the bottom rack of your dishwasher. This releases glass-protecting agents to neutralize damaging corrosive elements in every wash. It remains active for up to 50 washes and is recommended by leading glass manufacturers.

5 KEEP HANDS LOVELY

Decant your favourite washing-up liquid (lime- and lemon-scented versions are particularly lovely) into a pretty bottle and keep a tube of hand cream next to it to remind yourself to pamper your hands afterwards.

6 REVITALIZE YOUR DISHWASHER

Each month run the machine empty on a short cycle with 2 cups vinegar in the detergent receptacle to brighten up a dull interior. Use a toothpick to remove food particles trapped in the spray arm. Clean cutlery racks, filters and seals regularly.

7 CRYSTAL-CLEAR GLASSES

Stack glasses in a dishwasher so they can't rub against each other, or use specialist glass racks from wine merchants. Place a cup of white vinegar in the lowest part of the dishwasher and run for 10 minutes. Stop the cycle, add a little detergent and then re-start to get glasses that sparkle.

8 NEW REVOLUTION

Dishwasher tablets combining detergent, rinse aid, salt and a revolutionary 'Glass Protector Action' are designed to protect crystal and glasses from corrosion. You can also buy ultra-concentrated detergents made from natural plant and salt ingredients. A 500-ml (16-fl oz) bottle will wash about 2,200 glasses.

9 BURNT OFFERINGS

Slightly dampen spots, sprinkle liberally with baking soda and leave overnight. Use a plastic scourer to remove the remains of any culinary disaster. Try this if you've spilt something on the base of the oven, too.

equipment

10 BEST FOR BOARDS

Protect wooden chopping (cutting) boards from splitting by rubbing with a little vegetable oil. To remove stains, scrub well with a stiff brush and hot water. Eliminate food odours by rubbing with salt (a natural disinfectant) and a cut lemon. Store the boards in an airy place.

11 CHOP, CHOP

Have two chopping (cutting) boards: one for meat, the other for vegetables. If you are chopping a mixture of raw and cooked meat, always scrub the board well after chopping raw meat.

12 SIEVES AND STRAINERS

Clean fine-mesh sieves and strainers with a nylon bristle brush, which won't scratch or distort the openings.

13 COORDINATE ACCESSORIES

Choose cute household accessories (oven gloves, aprons, tablecloths, tea towels and ironing board covers) in pretty floral prints. They will pretty up your kitchen and cleaning becomes more fun, too.

14 EGGSTRA CARE

Many ice cream and mayonnaise recipes call for raw eggs, so hygiene is crucial to avoid salmonella. Wash any specialist equipment, or mixing or serving bowls, with a hot solution of washing-up liquid and dry thoroughly before use.

15 FRYING TONIGHT

The lids of most deep-fat fryers are detachable and some are dishwasher-proof. Clean inside each time you change the oil with a plastic scouring pad and washing-up liquid, avoiding damage to the non-stick coating. Outside, wipe over with a damp cloth and non abrasive cleaner.

16 GUNGY GRIDDLES

When using a cast-iron pan for the first time, wash in soapy water, rinse and dry thoroughly first. Brush with cooking oil and heat slowly until hot but not smoking. Cool and wipe out before use. Afterwards, cool completely before washing or soaking carefully – any debris left will cause the pan to smoke.

17 JUST JUICE

Prevent fruit and vegetable pulp sticking and staining juicers by washing juice machines promptly. Clean with a kitchen brush or the brush provided, taking care round the grating sieve's sharp edges. Wipe the motor housing and treat stained plastic with a damp cloth and a mild solution of bleach or rub with vegetable oil and rinse well.

18 MICROWAVE MAGIC

For stubborn stains in the microwave, place a bowl of hot water in the microwave. Switch to HIGH for about five minutes. Stand for a few minutes and then remove. Wipe inside with a soft cloth. Get rid of odours by heating a container of lemon juice and water on HIGH.

19 PERFECTO PASTA

Never immerse pasta-makers in water or the machine will rust. Use a dry pastry brush to remove any remaining pasta dough. Wipe clean with vegetable oil or a slightly damp cloth.

20 PLASTIC PROTECTOR

After each use, scrub a plastic chopping (cutting_ board with a small brush, hot water and detergent (most are dishwasher-proof but check the manufacturers' recommendations). Wipe over with a mild solution of bleach to kill lingering bacteria.

21 PRISTINE PROCESSORS

Always unplug mixers and food processors before cleaning. Pushers, lids and bowls are usually dishwasher safe. Use a brush and hot soapy water to clean blades. Stains from carrots and spices can be removed by wiping with kitchen paper moistened with a little vegetable oil.

22 RUST REMOVER

To treat rust on metal baking dishes and cookware, sprinkle powdered detergent on the spot. Scour with the cut side of half a raw potato. Alternatively, pour coca-cola over the rust and leave it to work overnight. Wash off in the morning. Rust on iron or steel may be removed with steel wool.

23 CHUCK OUT CRUMBS

Once a week or so empty the crumbs in your toaster. Always unplug it first, turn it upside down and shake. Use a clean dry toothbrush to sweep away crumbs. On stainless steel, use the designated polish.

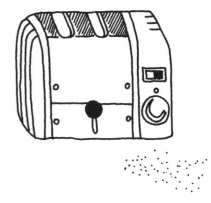

24 CAFETIERE CARE

First remove the plunger and unscrew the rod from the filter assembly. Wash the filter and glass beaker in hot soapy water or the dishwasher (if suitable). Buff brass or chrome frames with a soft cloth.

25 ESPRESSO CLEAN

Never try to force open the water tank lid of a cappuccino maker – wait until the pressure subsides just after use and it comes off easily. The steam/cappuccino nozzle is usually removable and can be washed by hand. If you have not used your machine for a while, check the nozzle before you switch it on – use a pin to unblock it, if necessary.

26 FRESHEN UP FILTERS

Unplug and allow electric coffee makers to cool down prior to cleaning. Wash the filter holder and nylon filters by hand in warm soapy water. Glass jugs are usually dishwasher-proof. Wipe the body of the machine with a damp cloth.

27 REGION BY REGION

In hard-water areas descale every eight to ten weeks and every six months where water is only moderately hard. Use proprietary descalers that state clearly that they are suitable for plastic kettles and/or coffee makers.

28 VINEGAR DESCALER

Cover the element of your kettle with a solution of half cold water, half distilled vinegar. Leave for a couple of hours then rinse, the liquid and discard.

food & drink

29 A PIECE OF CAKE

To keep cake from drying out and becoming stale, place half an apple inside the tin with it. Alternatively, fasten a slice of bread to the cut edge of the cake with cocktail sticks.

30 COOK'S HANDS

Remove strong food smells from your hands by rubbing them under cold running water while holding a stainless steel spoon in the same way as soap. Rinse with soap and water. Or try the perfumer's trick: dunk your hands in coffee grounds then wash with soap and water.

31 CLEAN UP AS YOU GO

To keep order in the kitchen when cooking or preparing food, clean up after each step. This will also help to prevent the transference of germs between cooked and raw ingredients.

32 PLASTIC PRODUCTS

Scrub stains with a paste of bicarbonate of soda and warm water. Heavier marks may be treated with a mix of 50 ml (2 fl oz) dishwasher detergent and 250 ml (8 fl oz) warm water (wear gloves or you could irritate your hands).

33 BOTTLE NECK

When sauce refuses to come out of the bottle, push a drinking straw right to the bottom and then take it out again. This adds enough air to get it flowing.

34 EGGSTRA, EGGSTRA

To check an egg for freshness, study the shell first. A fresh egg has a dull shell while a stale one will look glassy smooth. If in doubt, place the egg in a bowl of water. An egg that sinks to the bottom is fresh. If it floats, throw it away.

35 FISH FINGERS

If you've been preparing fish and want to remove the smell from your hands, wash them with toothpaste. Lemon juice and a little salt also work well – the salt sloughs away dead skin and softens your hands.

36 GOOD GRILLING

Cut a red onion in half, pierce it with a fork and dip in water. Use one onion half to wipe down the grill rack. This also helps reduce smoke and improves the flavour of food.

37 KEEP FRUIT & VEG FRESH

Wrap fruit and vegetables in newspaper before storing in the bottom of the fridge and they will last longer. Always store tomatoes at room temperature, however.

38 REDUCE LAST-MINUTE PANICS

Stock up with essentials so you'll always have something in the house. Tinned tomatoes, olive oil, pasta, sea salt and peppercorns, Parmesan, wine vinegar, garlic, stock and rice can all form the basis of a delicious supper.

39 RIPEN PEACHES & PEARS

Place pears in a paper bag with a ripe apple to ripen them. Quickly ripen peaches by placing them in a box and covering them with several sheets of newspaper.

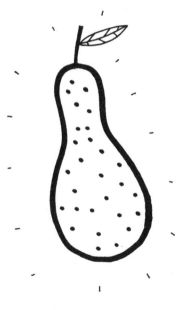

40 SALAD DAYS

Keep crisp leaves in the salad drawer of your fridge. Wash and pat dry or dressing won't cling to them. Dress salads at the last minute or the leaves will soon wilt.

41 SHOP TILL YOU DROP

Secure a piece of paper to your fridge with a magnet – use this to write down household items as you run out. Shop only after you've eaten to avoid buying food you don't need.

42 SMART COOKIE

Place a piece of blotting paper in the base of a biscuit jar or tin. Biscuits will stay fresh for longer.

43 SWEET SOLUTION

Honey can crystallize anywhere, whether you keep it on the shelf or in the fridge. While crystallization won't affect the quality of the product, it will make it harder to spread. Gently warm the pot in the microwave or a pan of heated water to restore runny honey.

44 HERBILICIOUS!

Grow herbs in a window box outside your kitchen or buy pots from supermarkets to keep indoors and you'll always be able to cook something interesting. Start your collection with basil, thyme, parsley, sage, tarragon and rosemary.

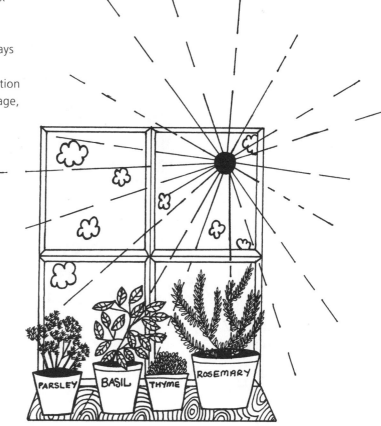

45 VIRTUAL SHOPPER

If you don't have time to go to the shops, use the Internet or order groceries from supermarkets with a delivery service. More specialist producers may deliver by overnight courier.

46 MAKE GARLIC DISAPPEAR

To remove garlic and onion smells from your hands, mix a ratio of two level tablespoons baking soda to a glass of water. Soak your hands for 30 seconds to a minute.

47 STUBBORN LIDS

When it's hard to open a jar, wrap a rubber band around the lid for a better grip. If this fails, run a little hot water over the lid.

48 AVOID ODOURS

If regular washing won't shift unpleasant smells in your thermos, pour in a few tablespoons of vinegar or bicarbonate of soda. Top up with hot water and leave for half an hour. Pour away the solution and then rinse thoroughly.

49 THERMOS FRESHENER

After each use, clean flasks with hot soapy water and a brush for bottles. Rinse well and air dry. Avoid getting water between the outer casing and inner insulating flask. Remove stubborn or hard-to-reach stains by first filling the flask with hot water. Drop in two denture-cleaning tablets and leave overnight. Rinse and air-dry.

50 VIBRANT VEGETABLES

Refresh green vegetables such as French beans and mangetouts in ice-cold water. This stops them overcooking and helps maintain their colour. Reheat quickly before serving.

51 GET PACKING

For perfect picnics, freeze drinks the night before – they'll stay cold the next day and will also help keep food chilled.

52 BUZZ OFF

Include some sprigs of fresh mint in a picnic basket when eating al fresco. Bees and wasps will stay away from your food if you place mint on the picnic blanket.

53 TRAVELLING WITH FOOD

Transport food in an ice-filled cooler and inside an air-conditioned car, if you're driving, not the boot (trunk). Throw away food that's been in the cooler for more than an hour.

54 STAIN-FREE TUPPERWARE

Tupperware stains can be bleached out by strong sunlight. In the summer, put your plastic containers in the garden and leave for several hours in the sun. Alternatively, to remove red stains, apply mustard overnight and then wash well.

freezers & fridges

55 BREAK THE ICE

To defrost a freezer, unplug and place bowls of hot, not boiling, water inside. Use a wooden spoon to scrape ice away. Remove stains with neat bicarbonate of soda on a damp cloth. Wipe clean and dry.

56 FELT-TIP PENS ON FRIDGES

If your children have been scribbling on the fridge (or worktops or furniture) you may be able to remove wet stains with a damp cloth. Otherwise wipe with a clean cloth dampened with methylated spirits. Rinse thoroughly afterwards.

57 SMEAR-FREE DOORS

Stainless steel doors on fridges and other appliances can easily become marked and covered in fingerprints. Remove them quickly and easily with a little baby oil on a paper towel. This also works to remove glue from labels or stickers.

58 LOCATION, LOCATION

Place your fridge in a cool part of the kitchen away from direct sun and not beside the oven or other hotter appliances. Make sure there's good circulation around the coils and for maximum efficiency, dust them regularly.

59 FRESHEN UP

Tuck an eggcup of bicarbonate of soda away on one of the shelves of your fridge to remove bad smells and change once a month. Wipe down the inside with a solution of 1 part bicarbonate of soda to 7 parts water or use a damp cloth sprinkled with a few drops of vanilla essence.

60 SAVE ENERGY

Replace your freezer with an energy-efficient one to save money on your bills. Check that the door seals are working and avoid leaving the door open for long periods of time.

61 SEAL IT

The longer you leave a fridge door open, the more it will warm up inside. To prevent mould forming on door seals, wipe over from time to time with white vinegar.

glasses & dishware

63 PERFECTLY STYLED

Invest in a set of flutes for champagnes and sparkling wines and large glasses for red and white wine. Matching sets make for a neat table. Avoid deep coloured glasses – it's impossible to gauge how much you've had to drink!

64 BANISH BLACK SPECKS

Apply a little baking soda to a damp cloth and rub the spot to get rid of black specks on china. Or try non-gel toothpaste on a plastic scouring brush.

65 HIGH & DRY

Avoid breaking china by buying a drying rack. Dishes, plates and cups will be evenly spaced so they won't clash against each other. What's more, you can display them in the rack and save time stashing them away in cupboards.

62 FRIDGE HYGIENE

Store cooked foods above uncooked ones in your fridge. This minimizes the risk of food poisoning caused by drips from uncooked foods. Wrap any food with strong odours and avoid storing close to dairy foods that may taint. And throw away that slimy lettuce at the back or it could contaminate other foods!

66 WORKS A TREAT

To remove wax from glass and dishes, heat it with a hair dryer then wipe with a clean cloth. Continue to wipe and polish with used fabric softener sheets and then wash as normal in hot soapy water.

67 CLEANER CHINA

Mugs and cups left with tea or coffee inside for too long can become stained, so scrub them with a little baking soda and a damp cloth. Toothpaste will do the same trick.

68 CHOOSING CHINA

Plain, striped and patterned china in the same colour looks good together. Or try a theme such as 1950s, animal prints, willow patterns or a mix of pretty florals for vintage-style chic.

69 SIMPLE SHELF-LINERS

Buy lengths of colourful felt or baize cut to the same size as your shelf tops. Secure with strong adhesive and you'll have a non-slip surface on which to place china and glass.

70 BRIGHTEN UP

Alka-Seltzer isn't just good for curing hangovers – dissolve a tablet in warm water at the base of a vase to remove stains and leave it shiny-new.

71 WHITE WORKS

It's true – white always looks elegant. Mix and match textures – grouped together a white collection can be wonderful and it's often cheaper. Look out for bargains in catering suppliers.

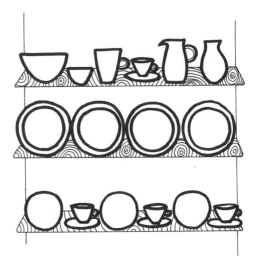

72 GET IN THE GROOVE

Hand-wash cut-glass crystal individually in warm soapy water and use a toothbrush to get into all the grooves. Rinse in warm water with lemon juice for extra shine and dry with a linen tea towel.

73 DECANT IT!

Fill the base of a glass decanter with hot (not boiling) water and washing-up liquid. Sprinkle in some coarse sand and swill it around to loosen any sediment. Rinse in hot water and pat dry with kitchen towel. To remove moisture inside, roll up a tube of kitchen paper slightly longer than the bottle, leave overnight and remove.

74 GOOD ALL-ROUNDER

For a cleaner that's ideal for glass and silver, mix together 4 litres (7 pints) hot water, 100 ml (3 ½ fl oz) household ammonia, 100 ml (3 ½ fl oz) white vinegar and 200 g (7 oz) bicarbonate of soda together. Store in a tightly sealed bottle.

75 A TOUCH OF SPARKLE

For glasses that gleam, fill a sink with plenty of hot (but not too hot) soapy water and add a dash of vinegar before you wash them. Polish immediately afterwards with a soft cloth (preferably linen) to avoid watermarks forming round the rims.

76 DISHWASHER SAFE

Some glazed items (mugs, vases and plates) have been fired at more than 600 °C (111 °F) so they can stand any heat encountered in your dishwasher. Most pieces will withstand a scrubber sponge or steel wool pad.

77 SMASHING!

Avoid using too-hot water to wash glasses and take care when mixing temperatures. If you wash a glass in hot water and then rinse it in very cold water, it will crack. Try not to overload the sink with glasses.

78 TEA-LEAF TRICK

Fill a stained decanter half-full of warm soapy water to which a few tea-leaves have been added. Soak, shaking well at intervals. Empty and rinse thoroughly.

79 CRYSTAL CLEAN

Use a paste of lemon juice and baking powder to remove small stains from crystal. Treat tougher stains by placing 2 teaspoons uncooked rice inside the crystal piece, add water and swirl.

80 PERFECTLY PRESERVED

Clean the inside of brass preserving pans with a paste made from vinegar and kitchen salt. Wash and rinse thoroughly before cooking; dry well. Metal polish may be used on the outside but never use this inside any pan intended for cooking.

81 HANDLE WITH CARE

Prevent breakages by washing porcelain in a bowl or sink lined with a towel or rubber mat. Fired at high temperatures, porcelain is glass-like, so use a mild solution of washing-up liquid and warm water. Wipe with a soft cloth and use a soft toothbrush to get to all the nooks and crannies. Rinse well in clean water.

82 WIPE CLEAN

Some pottery is painted with acrylic and then treated with a spray-on glaze that won't withstand washing in water. To clean, simply wipe with a damp cloth. Antique pottery can be dusted with a soft brush provided nothing is flaking loose on the surface.

83 POROUS POTTERY

Unglazed pottery such as terracotta is porous so it will soak up water. Wash with warm water and washing-up liquid. It may take a day or two for the pot to dry out.

keep it fresh

84 NATURAL MATERIALS

Vacuum wastepaper bins made of cardboard, wicker, paper, straw or wood with the small brush attachment. Wipe away marks with a damp cloth dipped in warm soapy water – avoid harsh cleaners that will eat away at the surface.

85 HERBAL REMEDY

For a fresh Mediterranean fragrance, tie crushed herbs in bunches and hang on the walls of your kitchen. Replace often to avoid dust. Place chopped fresh herbs in ice-cube trays, fill with water and then freeze – use as much as you want in sauces and stews, when you want.

86 ODOUR EATER

Boil 100 ml (3½ fl oz) vinegar with 1 litre (1¾ pints) of water. The rising heat carries vinegar particles to surfaces on which cooking grease and smoke have landed and neutralizes their effect.

87 STOP LINGERING SMELLS

Switch on the extractor 10–15 minutes before you start cooking. Run it for a few minutes afterwards to get rid off cooking smells (some extractors automatically switch off after a set time).

88 KEEP BINS SMELLING SWEET

Wash and deodorize bins with a solution of 1 teaspoon lemon juice to 1 litre (1¾ pints) water. Sprinkling baking soda into the base of every rubbish bag will also keep smells at bay.

89 CLEAR COOKING SMELLS

While a house full of food smells sounds wonderful, it's the ones that linger that can be unpleasant. After cooking, open windows and turn on the extractor fan (if you have one) to combat food smells.

91 RECYCLE IT

Save money and waste by recycling plastic supermarket bags as bin liners. Paper bags can also be used for dry rubbish and newspapers to be recycled.

92 TIME-SAVING TIP

Empty the kitchen bin and mix up a cleaner-and-water solution inside. Now mop the floor. While you're mopping away the dirt in the bin will loosen. Drain and scrub with a stiff brush, rinse in running water and dry with a cloth.

93 AVOID BUILD-UP

To keep your waste disposal working efficiently, grind small amounts of food at a time. After you've finished, run a steady, rapid flow of cold (not hot) water for up to 30 seconds. Hot water will solidify fat and greasy waste.

90 FRUIT SCENTS

Spray napkins with a lime-scented linen spray, which won't compete with the food. As guests unfold them, the scent is subtly released. Light a grapefruit scented candle to cut through any lingering cooking odours, freshen up the air and lift the mood.

94 FAT-BUSTER

Fatty wastes can build up inside a waste disposer so from time to time grind a handful of ice cubes with bicarbonate of soda. Together they will safely scour the inside of your unit.

95 GOING AWAY?

If no one's going to be home for a few days, make sure food waste that could start to smell is not left in the disposal unit. To flush away any remains, plug the sink, fill with around 5 cm (2 in) of water and run the disposer while the water drains.

96 A TOUCH OF ZEST

One quick and easy way to deodorize your waste disposal unit is to grind orange or lemon peel inside it every so often.

97 USE STRONG SACKS

Be scrupulous: only put items securely tied in plastic bags inside your outside bin otherwise if you get a split, you'll have to disinfect each week. Hosing down is an easy option, or place beside an outside drain and rinse around the base and sides with a solution of 40 ml (1¼ fl oz) bleach to 5 litres (1.3 gallons) of water. Wash the lid in the same way and invert to dry.

98 DON'T DO IT!

Never pour oil or grease through your waste disposal or grind large bones (small ones are safe, though and can even help break up grease deposits). Avoid grinding bulky, fibrous foods such as sweetcorn kernels and never pour caustic soda or chemical drain cleaners into the unit.

pots & pans

99 CAST-IRON COATING

Wash uncoated cast iron by hand, not in a dishwasher. Dry thoroughly. Prevent rusting by brushing the surface with a thin layer of vegetable oil.

100 NON-STICK SEASONING

Wash, rinse and dry new non-stick pans prior to use. Lightly season the coating by brushing a thin layer of vegetable oil inside. Re-season after dishwashing. Use a scourer designed for non-stick surfaces (never a metal or abrasive one) to remove burnt-on food.

101 COPPER CARE

Wash copper pans in a hot solution of washing-up liquid. Clean as brass (see tip 109). Afterwards, wash thoroughly.

102 ENAMEL PROTECTOR

Wash enamel pans in hot washing-up liquid and dry at once to prevent a white film forming on the surface. If thinly coated, food may stick and burn, so soak the pan and use a nylon scourer to remove it. Marks on stained, worn enamel may be removed by boiling up a solution of biological washing powder inside. Rinse thoroughly afterwards.

103 OVER THE RAINBOW

Wash stainless steel pots by hand or in a dishwasher. Over time rainbow markings may develop – remove these with proprietary stainless steel cleaner. Too-high heat can cause brown marks on the outside so apply a proprietary cleaner. Boil a solution of biological washing powder (1 tbsp to 1 litre (1¾ pint) water) for 10 minutes to tackle severely burnt-on bits of food. Repeat if necessary and wash thoroughly.

104 PERFECTLY POLISHED

Use lemon juice or a slice of lemon sprinkled with baking soda to brighten up brass and copper. Rub with a soft cloth, rinse with water and dry. Or try half a lemon dipped in salt. Rinse and buff dry with a soft cloth – this method can lighten copper.

105 VERDIGRIS VENEER

A proprietary rust remover will remove heavy, green corrosion from brass or copper. Apply with a paintbrush and use fine steel wool to gently rub the surface. Clean with metal polish.

106 SQUEAKY CLEAN

Before cleaning a wok, season first (see below). After cooking, wipe out with a damp cloth. Scrubbing a seasoned wok ruins the careful patina created by seasoning. If the wok becomes rusty, however, wash and season again. Treat electric woks according to the manufacturer's advice.

107 IT'S THE SEASON

Almost non-stick, a well-seasoned wok needs just a light clean and lasts for years. Once washed, heat on a burner until a few drops of water sprinkled on the surface start to dance (the wok will become darker). Once black dip paper towel wads in sesame oil. Hold with a pair of tongs and wipe over the surface. Reduce the heat to low and leave the wok to sit for 15 minutes. Turn off the heat and cool. Repeat before cooking.

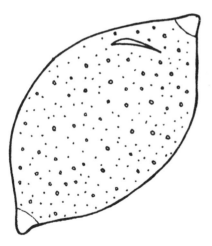

108 RHUBARB, RHUBARB

Wash uncoated aluminium by hand, never in a dishwasher. Remove black tarnish by boiling up acidic foods such as rhubarb or a cut lemon with water. Wash thoroughly afterwards. Clean hard-anodized aluminium in hot soapy water. Brownish film may be removed with an abrasive cleaner.

109 SOAPY SOLUTION

Wash copper and brass in a warm solution of washing-up liquid with a soft cloth. Rinse and dry with another cloth. Apply cream or polish with a soft cloth and buff before the polish has dried. Treat heavier tarnishing with copper or brass wadding impregnated with polish – use occasionally as this is quite an abrasive method as well as being messy and hard work.

110 GLASS-CERAMIC CARE

Soak pans made of glass or ceramic in warm washing-up liquid to remove burnt-on food and then apply a nylon scourer. Rinse afterwards.

111 THE RIGHT STUFF

Authentic woks are made from carbon steel. Always clean a new one before cooking to remove the manufacturer's protective coating. Scrub inside and out with washing-up liquid and steel wool; rinse with hot water. If any coating remains, fill with water and boil until the coating dissolves. Empty and scrub again with steel wool and soap.

silver, steel, pewter & tin

112 DON'T MIX IT!

Never combine silver and stainless steel cutlery in a dishwasher or the silver will turn black. Black spots will also appear if you allow dishwasher detergent to come into contact with silver. Remove silver cutlery from the dishwasher immediately the cycle has come to a close and dry at once to avoid stains and pitting from salt residue.

113 COCKTAIL STICK TRICK

Used frequently, candlesticks and candelabra can build up a body of wax. Avoid damage to the silver by leaving it in a warm room to soften the wax. Lay on a soft cloth and slowly and carefully remove the wax with a blunt cocktail stick. Buff with a silver polishing cloth.

POLISH

114 FAMILY SILVER

Stains on silver can be removed by dissolving a little salt in lemon juice. Dip a soft cloth into the mixture and rub the cutlery. Rinse in warm water and finish by buffing to a shine with a chamois.

115 HANDLE WITH CARE

Never leave ivory, wood, horn or bone handles to soak in water. Instead, stand the metal parts only in a jar of hot washing-up water. Wipe handles with a hot, damp cloth and pat dry with a clean cloth.

116 STEELY SECRETS

Steel wool can scratch stainless steel and acidic or salty foods may cause pit marks. To avoid, rinse stainless steel soon after use and wash in hot soapy water. Remove baked-on food with a paste of bicarbonate of soda and water.

117 CHALK IT UP

To prevent silver cutlery from tarnishing, place a few pieces of chalk in the drawer with it to absorb moisture.

118 CANDLESTICK CARE

Avoid placing silver candlesticks in the freezer to remove wax. Sudden temperature changes can cause silver to react dramatically, especially if it's made of more than one metal as metals may react at different rates causing the candlestick to split apart.

119 DIY DIP

Line a washing-up bowl with foil. Fill with very hot water and add a handful of washing soda. Immerse tarnished silver so that it is in contact with the foil. Turn large items that fall above the water line after five minutes. Do not immerse for more than 10 minutes. Replace foil when it darkens.

120 USE IT OR LOSE IT

To keep silver at its best, use it every day – constant use gives a rich and mellow lustre. Store in tarnish-inhibiting cloth and acid-free tissue paper. Don't use rubber bands to secure the wrapping, though: rubber can corrode silver through several layers of cloth causing permanent damage.

121 GENTLY DOES IT

Dust silver with impregnated silver polishing cloths and mitts – it is a soft metal so don't rub too hard or you could scratch the surface. Work in straight, even strokes. Never rub crosswise or with a rotary movement.

122 PERFECTLY FOILED

To revitalize tarnished silver cutlery, place a piece of aluminium foil in a plastic bucket. Sprinkle over 3 tablespoons bicarbonate of soda. Put the silver on top and cover with hot water. Leave until the mixture stops bubbling. Rinse and polish with a dry cloth.

123 SILVER PLATE CARE

Wash silver plate cutlery soon after use. Certain foods leave stains that are harder to remove the longer you leave them. Treat as silver, but polish with less vigour – plating is softer. Don't use dip solutions on plate that has become patchy and never leave silver-plated items in dip for more than ten minutes.

124 ASK A PROFESSIONAL

Antique pewter should always be maintained by a professional – polishing at home decreases its value. Check for relevant organizations on the Internet or go on personal recommendation.

125 PERK UP

Once a year clean pewter with warm soapy water and a soft cloth. If heavily marked, apply silver or brass polish and a soft cloth. Treat severe corrosion with metal polish and ultra-fine steel wool. Buff with a soft cloth.

126 RUST REMOVER

Rub tin with extra-fine steel wool and once the rust has disappeared, wash in a soapy solution. Rinse well and dry completely. Apply a thin coat of car wax to prevent the rust from returning.

127 INTRICATE PIECES

If you are cleaning a piece with delicate engraving or ridges, use a soft toothbrush to remove the last traces of silver polish – any residue looks ugly.

**TOOTHY SHINE**

Place toothpaste on a soft cloth and use it to rub solid silver (not silver-plate) and then rinse it off gently. Don't use whitening toothpaste – it can damage the surface.

SCRATCHED SILVER

Silver is a soft metal so to lessen the chance of scratches, avoid placing it beside abrasive objects. A silversmith can buff it up and remove any scratches and dents. The disadvantage is that the silver becomes a little more worn each time this is done.

130 POLISHING METHODS

Manufacturers of fine silver services recommend creams and liquids for medium tarnishing. Dry to a fine, powdery deposit and buff with a dry cloth. Or try foaming silver paste applied with a damp sponge to form a film. Rinse in water and dry thoroughly.

131 TARNISHED TIN PREVENTION

Use a feather duster to clean tin with elaborate decoration or wipe with a dry or slightly damp cloth. Wash in a mild solution of washing-up liquid and warm water with a soft cloth. Abrasive scrubbing brushes and cleaners are too harsh and may scratch through the plating and so cause rust.

sinks

132 ACRYLIC BRIGHTENER

Watermarks may be removed from an acrylic sink with white vinegar. Never use an abrasive cleanser or scourer on acrylic or you risk scratches.

133 IT'S A STEAL!

Neat detergent removes stains from stainless steel. Avoid abrasive cleaners or scourers if you are concerned about scratches. Add shine by polishing with methylated spirits and a dry cloth.

134 ENAMEL ENHANCERS

Remove stains from enamel with a paste of bicarbonate of soda and hydrogen peroxide (gentle bleach). Rub in and leave to dry, then rinse off. Or try a mix of borax and a cut lemon. Do not use scourers or bleach on enamel.

135 BABY OIL BRILLIANCE

Restore lustre to chrome trim on taps and kitchen appliances by polishing with baby oil and a soft cloth. Remove any rust spots with crumpled-up foil.

136 SINK SIZZLER

To unblock a sink, pour 1 cup of bicarbonate of soda down the drain. Slowly pour in the same amount of white vinegar. The reaction makes a sizzling sound. Follow with water and repeat as necessary. Place a plunger over the drain hole, push down and then up rapidly.

137 KITCHEN SINK DRAMA

For a spectacular finish, wipe round an aluminium sink with a solution of diluted bleach and pat dry with kitchen paper. Buff with more paper and baby oil for a gleaming sink.

storage & shelves

138 GOOD CLEAR OUT

Every so often go through cupboards, check expiry dates on cans and packages. Throw away out-of-date items. Not only does this avoid clutter – it's healthier too. Items such as rice and flour can attract other occupants.

139 ON DISPLAY

The advantage of open shelving is that everything is within easy reach but only have it for the crockery and glasses you use regularly or dust will accumulate.

140 BAMBOO & WILLOW

Wipe clean with a solution of washing-up liquid and dry with a cloth. Willow is mainly used for hampers and similar baskets. It is unsealed so do not over-wet or leave to soak.

141 PORTABLE PRODUCTS

Fill a portable basket or trug with cleaning essentials such as polish, dusters, cloths and window spray. Cleaning's so much easier when everything is to hand.

**PERFECT PANS**

Stack saucepans in deep drawers or a
corner cupboard with their lids upside
down. Or hang them on metal hooks over a
work surface; fix hooks and shelves that will
withstand the weight.

143 BASKET STAIN REMOVER

When regular washing won't work, apply
gentle bleach to baskets and re-varnish if
necessary. If the stain is still there, apply
coloured polyurethane wood varnish to
disguise it.

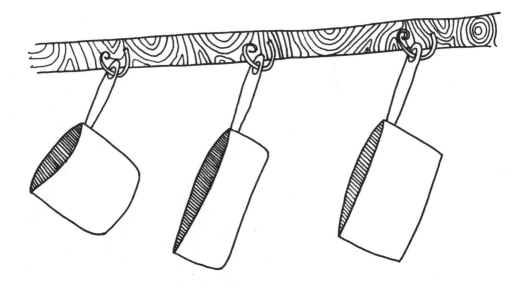

144 STEPPING OUT

Safety first – keep a small stepladder in a kitchen cupboard. It's perfect when you want to dust down a tall shelf or get out the family china for a special celebration.

145 SODA SPARKLER

Dust exteriors of units with a clean cloth and wipe with a damp cloth – avoid abrasive scouring brushes. Remove marks on shelves by sprinkling with bicarbonate of soda and wiping over with a damp cloth.

146 RAISE A GLASS

To prevent glasses becoming dusty, place them upside down on shelves. Arrange in order of size so they are easier to find and to avoid breakages.

147 TREAT CANE KINDLY

Imported baskets are mostly made of split cane with a light seal or varnish. Wipe down with water. Heavier dirt can be removed with a solution of washing-up liquid – anything harsher breaks down the seal and damages the cane below.

148 SHINE ON

Clean wood cabinets with a little washing-up liquid applied directly with another cloth. Rinse with water and dry with a cloth. Once a year apply a thin coat of car wax to the surface, then buff. Spray a paper towel with glass cleaner to wipe down windows – if you spray directly onto the glass you risk damaging the surrounding wood.

149 WICKER WORK

Use wire cutters to trim broken wicker. To clean, spritz with a plastic spray filled with water and one tablespoon vinegar and then wipe clean, using a cotton bud for crevices. If possible, dry outdoors in the sun; keep away from direct heat sources indoors.

stoves

150 CHEER UP CHROME

Oven rings made of chrome often become sticky. Shine them up with a paste of vinegar and cream of tartar.

151 STOVE-TOP SPILLAGES

Prevent build-up by wiping down every time you use the stove. Avoid abrasive cleaners on enamel and stainless steel. To remove encrusted stains, apply caustic cleaner with an old toothbrush. Leave for a few hours then scrub away with hot water.

152 MAKE IT EASY

One simple way to clean the oven is to place a bowl of water inside. Heat on a high temperature for 20 minutes to loosen dirt and grease. Wipe away condensation with a cloth or paper towel. Afterwards use a cloth to smear a thin paste of bicarbonate of soda and water on enamel linings. This dries to a protective layer that absorbs greasy soiling and makes it easier to clean next time.

153 TLC FOR OVENS

As an alternative to commercial cleaner, wet the surface of the oven and sprinkle with bicarbonate of soda. Rub with fine steel wool and wipe away residue with a damp cloth. Repeat as necessary. Rinse well and dry. Do this every two weeks.

154 DIVINE DOORS

Remove cooked-on food from doors with a metal spatula or ceramic hob scraper followed by spray-on cleaner. Removable glass can be soaked in a solution of biological washing powder.

155 GOOD GRILLING

Ideally wash the grill after each use in hot water and detergent. If you're faced with a build-up of grease, scrape out solids with a spatula, wipe out with balls of newspaper and then wash as before.

156 SPARKLING SHELVES

Soak oven shelves overnight in 4 parts hot water to 1 part biological washing powder. If they are too large for your sink, place in the bath. They'll be much easier to clean the next day.

157 A PINCH OF SALT

If you have spilt something in the oven, do some damage limitation. While the oven is still warm, dampen the spill slightly and sprinkle on a little salt. Once cooled, scrape away the spill and wash clean.

158 SPILT SUGAR

If you spill sugar on a hob, turn off the heat at once. Remove the pan and wipe the glass with a damp cloth before you continue cooking. If left, sugar crystallizes as it cools and this can cause pitting. Protect glass hobs with proprietary hob conditioner.

work surfaces

159 ADD LUSTRE TO LAMINATE

Disinfect laminate with a few drops of eucalyptus oil. Tough marks may be removed with a sprinkling of neat washing detergent. Leave for a few minutes and then rinse (do not scour).

160 MAKE LIFE EASIER

If you are buying a new kitchen and want quick and easy work surfaces avoid high maintenance stone, marble and granite and have engineered stone instead. This often resembles granite but does not require a sealant and needs very little extra care.

161 BUTCHER'S BLOCKS

Brighten a butcher's block with a paste made from salt and a few drops of lemon juice. With a cleaning cloth rub hard enough into the wood to free food particles. Rinse and wipe clean for a fresh-smelling alternative. Or scrub with 10 ml (⅓ fl oz) household bleach mixed with 2 litres (3½ pints) water. Rinse away the excess and take care not to saturate the wood.

162 CHROME CLEANSER

Apply a mix of white vinegar and salt on a soft cloth to chrome. Rinse well with water and buff to brilliance with a dry cloth. Half a lemon lightly dipped in salt will do the same job.

163 CLEAN SLATE

Add shine to slate by wiping it with a few drops of lemon oil. Polish with a soft dry cloth. To remove oil stains, sprinkle with a liberal amount of flour and leave for 10 minutes. Scrub with a grease-cutting cleaner or warm water and washing-up liquid. Oil worktops once or twice a year with 50-50 boiled linseed oil and turpentine. buff till dry.

164 ALL-PURPOSE CLEANER

For a cleaner that's perfect for use on work surfaces and throughout the house, mix 2 heaped tablespoons bicarbonate of soda with 1 tablespoon white vinegar. Store in an airtight container.

165 SPRUCE UP STEEL

Remove hard-water spots from stainless steel by polishing with a clean dry cloth. Stubborn spots can be removed with a cloth soaked in neat vinegar. Avoid abrasive cleaners – they will dull the finish and can even cause rusting.

166 BAKE UP

Try cleaning kitchen surfaces with a paste of baking powder and water – they'll come up clean without any toxic fumes. Stubborn stains, such as rust marks from wet cast-iron saucepans, soon disappear.

167 TILE REFRESHER

To remove splashes and stains from kitchen tiles, use a cut lemon to rub salt on them. This also works on scorch marks and stains on unsealed wood.

168 NATURAL ABRASIVES

Avoid harsh abrasives on plastic laminates such as Formica. Instead use a sponge and all-purpose kitchen cleaner. Sprinkle obstinate stains with bicarbonate of soda and rub with a soft damp cloth. Rinse and dry with a clean cloth. Or make a paste from cream of tartar and lemon juice. Leave on the stain for 15 minutes. Rinse and dry.

169 NON-TOXIC STONE SEALANT

Countertops made of stone are sometimes sealed with a penetrating commercial sealant. Make sure that any surface on which you prepare food is sealed with a non-toxic sealant. Vegetable oil is an inexpensive option that is perfect for food preparation areas.

170 PROTECT STONE SURFACES

Marble, stone and granite are the most delicate worktop surfaces so always place coasters, trivets or place mats beneath glassware and dishes to prevent scratches. Never set anything hot on a marble surface.

171 SPLATTERS & SPLASHES

Worktops and hobs are susceptible to cooking oil stains. Wipe any splatters away with paper towels and then apply a moist sponge and a solution of 50-50 white vinegar and warm water.

172 STAINS ON STONE

Determine whether the stain is water-based (spilled fruit juice) or oil-based (mayonnaise). For water-based stains, pour hot water from the tap onto the stain and leave for a few minutes. Wipe away excess. Blot with paper towels and a heavy weight. Leave overnight. Repeat for oil-based stains but use acetone (don't heat). Again, leave overnight. Repeat as necessary.

173 CALCIUM CHOMPER

Stone can often be cleaned with a detergent and warm water but anything stronger may scratch or stain the surface. Never use vinegar, lemon or acidic cleaners on marble or limestone – the acid in them will eat away at the calcium in the stone.

174 SOLID SURFACE SYNTHETICS

It's fine to apply light abrasion to surfaces such as Corian. Use a damp scrubbing sponge sprinkled with mildly abrasive cleaner and apply gentle pressure. Rinse with a sponge then dry with a soft cloth.

175 UNSEALED WOOD

Preserve the beauty of wood by rubbing the surface with boiled linseed oil. Wipe away the excess with a soft cloth.

bathtubs & showers

176 ADD SPARKLE

To brighten showerheads, soak in vinegar for 20 minutes or brush with vinegar using an old toothbrush. A solution of washing-up liquid will clean shower screens.

177 DARN IT!

Unblock the holes in a showerhead that are clogged up with limescale deposits by piercing the holes with a darning needle. Finish by rinsing out the head with white vinegar.

178 LICK LIMESCALE

If your showerhead is coated in mineral deposits, here's an effortless way to clean it in two hours or less. Remove and soak for a few hours in a mix of 50/50 water and humidifier cleaner. You need just enough solution to cover the face of the showerhead. Rinse well and reattach.

178 AVOID ABRASIVES

Don't use abrasive cleaners on baths, basins or shower trays – they're much too harsh. Clean enamel baths, shower trays and basins with cream cleaner applied with a cloth and rinse well. Tackle acrylic baths with mild detergent solution.

180 CITRUS SCENT

Add a couple of drops of lemon essential oil to the final rinse when cleaning baths. It kills germs and it's deliciously scented, too.

181 BLITZ BATH STAINS

White vinegar is perfect for tough, hard-to-shift stains and its disinfectant properties make it an amazing all-round cleaner. Remove stubborn bath stains with a 1:5 solution of white vinegar and water.

182 MAGIC AWAY MOULD

If your shower sprouts mould, wipe down the walls with a solution of 1 teaspoon water softener, 1 tablespoon ammonia and 1 tablespoon vinegar in 200 ml (7 fl oz) warm water. Rinse with fresh water and buff dry.

183 ON THE SPOT

It's far simpler to clean a bath while it's warm so try cleaning it when you climb out of it. Keep a spray bottle of proprietary cleaner to hand and spritz this around immediately after use. Leave for a few minutes before rinsing off.

184 TIME FOR A DRINK

No, not you! Rid glass shower doors and screens of stains and lime scale by wiping them over with a glass of white wine.

185 SCRATCHES & STAINS

Rub half a lemon over a stubborn stain to make it disappear. Any scratches can be removed with silver polish. Rust stains may be removed with a paste made from borax and lemon juice.

186 MIRACLE MOULD REMOVER

To get rid of mould from sealant round baths, shower trays and basins, first clean the area with a solution of neat vinegar and then wipe over the top with a paste made from bicarbonate of soda and a little water.

187 BLUE RINSE

Cure blue-green stains on baths and showers caused by water with a high copper content with a paste of equal amounts of cream of tartar and bicarbonate of soda. Rub into the stain, leave for half an hour and rinse well with water. Repeat, if necessary.

188 CRACKED BATH SEALANT

Gently scrape away the existing sealant and make sure surfaces are clean and dry. Protect the wall and bath, sink or basin by masking off with tape. Apply new sealant in the gap pressing down with a wet spatula, if necessary. After five minutes remove the tape. Leave until completely dry, about 24 hours.

189 SPARKLING SHOWER SCREENS

Brighten up your shower screen by wiping it over once a week with a solution of washing-up liquid. Rinse down and buff with a soft cloth.

190 TIDEMARK TACKLE

Get rid of ugly tidemarks on baths and basins by applying neat liquid laundry detergent. Rinse off with warm water. Foam bath helps reduce the amount of scum left behind in the bath in the first place.

191 WASH & BRUSH UP

Clear soap scum effortlessly away from shower doors by wiping them with a used (dry) dryer sheet. It gets the job done quickly.

192 AVOID SCALDS

Reduce your hot-water temperature at the source or install thermostatically controlled mixer taps (faucets) to avoid dangerously hot water. If you have children, childproof hot taps can be fitted.

193 ON THE SPOT

Steam from a hot shower loosens grime so run the shower beforehand. Try cleaning with 60 ml (2 ½ fl oz) dishwasher detergent with 500 ml (17 fl oz) warm water mixed in a spray bottle. Wearing rubber gloves, spray liberally on walls then scrub with a sponge.

194 TRY MULTI-TASKING

Choose a bubble bath that cleans the bath
as you bathe so you can linger for longer.
Luxurious bath oils often leave grimy
tidemarks. To remove stubborn stains, soak
cotton wool or tissues in white spirit and
leave for an hour or so before rubbing
the marks away.

195 TEST FIRST

Avoid surface damage – test new products in inconspicuous areas first. Also avoid mixing bathroom cleaners – chlorine bleach and ammonia are an especially dangerous combination. But you can use more than one type of cleaner provided you rinse well between applications.

196 CURTAIN CLEANSER

If your shower curtain has seen better days, wash according to the care label but add a cup each of vinegar and bleach to the machine – it will look like new. Remove curtains as soon as the cycle is complete and hang back in position to drip-dry and remove any creases.

197 SHOWER CURTAIN PROTECTORS

Avoid leaving a shower curtain bunched up after use, especially in a small bathroom – the steam encourages mildew. If small spots of mildew appear, dab with bicarbonate of soda on a damp cloth. Wash larger areas in hot detergent, rub in lemon juice and dry in the sun, if possible.

198 FIT A FLOW RESTRICTOR

Avoid wasting water by fitting a flow restrictor to your shower. For optimum flow and to save water, restrict it to 6 litres (10½ pints) a minute. Flow restrictors are suitable for mains and power showers.

199 WASH AWAY WATERMARKS

Proprietary lime scale remover will also get rid of hard watermarks. Alternatively, use white vinegar or lemon juice.

200 WATER CONSERVATION

Take a refreshing shower instead of a bath. Did you know that a five-minute shower uses 35 litres (9.2 gallons) of water compared to a bath that uses 80 litres (21 gallons)? Over a week you could save over 300 litres (79 gallons) of water.

201 PREVENTION IS BETTER

To prevent plug-hole blockages, use a hair trap. If a drain becomes blocked, fill the sink with water, hold a rag in the overflow outlet and then plunge the drain.

202 REVAMP RUNNERS

Treat shower door runners to a scrub with white toothpaste and an old toothbrush. Rinse by brushing with vinegar. Or dip a stiff-bristled paintbrush in vinegar and scrub thoroughly.

203 NO SLIP-UPS

Shower curtains and screens keep the bathroom floor dry, but use non-slip mats in showers and baths and install side grips and rails for extra safety in the bath, especially if anyone in your home is elderly.

204 HAIRY FRIENDS

Contrary to popular belief, spiders do not come up through plug holes so keeping the plug in won't keep them out! To remove a spider, hang a roll of toilet paper over the side of the bath to give the spider an escape route.

205 MAD WHIRL

Most whirlpools and spas are self-draining but you need to clean out scum left in the pipe work. Once a week fill the bath with water and add a cupful of mild sterilizing liquid. Leave to circulate for five minutes. Empty the bath, refill with clean water and circulate for five minutes more to rinse.

décor & ambience

206 A GOOD CLEAR OUT

Empty bathroom cabinets regularly
– dispose of old cosmetics and medicines
carefully and keep them out of kids' reach.
Wipe out with soapy water then rinse
clean. For fun, paint a vibrant colour inside
cupboards to contrast with the walls.

207 SPACE SAVER

Make a small bathroom appear larger by
choosing smaller units. A smaller bath, sink
and toilet will add space and give the illusion
of the room being bigger than it really is.

208 ON THE SHELF

Store pretty bath oils and scrubs on glass
shelving either beside or at one end of the
bath to give you easy access to items you
need when bathing.

209 CALMING CANDLES

Buy one or two luxurious scented candles so that you can enjoy a candle-lit bath at the end of a busy day. Layer the fragrance with delicious matching bath oil to lighten your mood instantly.

210 GO FOR GLASS

Give the illusion of space by fitting narrow glass shelves beside or at one end of the bath or shower. Keep them gleaming with a solution of white vinegar.

211 ELEGANT SOLUTION

Consider placing a roll-top bath with legs in a small bathroom. Although this may seem to use up valuable space, seeing the floor underneath creates the illusion of space.

212 NATURAL DEODORIZER

Freshen up with this quick and easy trick. Add a few drops of vanilla extract to a cotton wool ball and leave this in the bathroom. Replace whenever the fragrance starts to fade.

213 PICTURE THIS

Your bathroom is the one place where you really lie back and contemplate the walls so add an elegant mirror, an interesting piece of art or a collection of carefully arranged shells.

214 STOCK UP

Store toilet rolls in a basket beside the toilet, or arrange them on a small shelf that is painted to match the wall – white works well.

sinks

215 FLOUR POWER

If your chrome taps (faucets) are less than sparkly, try rubbing them with flour. Rinse and buff with a soft cloth.

216 GET THEM GLEAMING

Apply paraffin to chrome taps (faucets) with a damp cloth – it dries almost instantly without drips and the smell soon disappears. The results are startling.

217 BE A CHEMIST

Acids mixed with alkalis create vigorous reactions. Pour half a cup of baking soda mixed with half a cup of vinegar down your sink for a quick and easy non-toxic pipe cleaner.

218 AVOID SOGGY SOAP SCUM

Prevent soap scum from clogging up basins by fitting a magnetic soap holder to the wall to keep the soap clean and dry. Alternatively, use soap that's stored in a pump-action container.

219 QUICK TIPPLE

Stainless steel can be quickly and easily cleaned with vodka. Place a little on a sponge or paper towel and wipe. Your taps (faucets) will soon be sparkling again so pour yourself a glass to celebrate!

220 HANDY SUPPLIES

Keep a frequently refreshed supply of hand towels and hand lotions next to the sink area to encourage cleanliness. A supply of surface wipes are good to keep in a drawer so the basin, taps and surrounding areas can be wiped clean easily.

221 SINKING FEELING

If your stainless steel sink is looking a
bit dull, rub the surface gently with a
scrunched-up ball of newspaper or sprinkle
it with baking powder, scrub and rinse off.

222 VERY VINEGAR

Use vinegar to clean your chrome taps
(faucets). The acid helps dissolve grime and
brings them up to a beautiful shine. But
don't try this on brass taps – or gold!

223 LINGERING LIMESCALE

From time to time rub taps with half a cut
lemon. Leave for a few minutes and then
wipe and buff dry to get rid of limescale
and add a fresh scent to your bathroom.

224 CARE WITH COLOUR

Wipe coloured sinks down with a damp
cloth and washing-up liquid solution.
Avoid staining by pouring diluted bleach
down the plug-hole but don't use this
elsewhere. Soak stubborn stains in a
solution of biological washing powder or
well-diluted bleach.

225 PERFECT PORCELAIN

Steel wool and scouring powders will
scratch porcelain so rub a freshly cut
lemon round the surface to cut through
grease and then rinse in running water.
Or sprinkle with bicarbonate of soda and
rub with a damp sponge. Neutralize with
a rinse of vinegar or lemon juice, then rinse
with running water.

226 LITTLE AND OFTEN

Wipe taps (faucets) often to remove traces
of toothpaste, etc. Diluted washing-up
liquid is gentler than all-purpose cleaner
and try working a toothbrush into all the
crevices. Ideally wipe and buff dry taps
(faucets) after every use.

tiles & surfaces

227 BRIGHTEN UP

For tiles that sparkle, sprinkle baking soda,
boracic acid or borax on the surface. Scrub
with a plastic mesh scrubber or sponge.

228 FIT AN EXTRACTOR

An extractor fan keeps moisture down so there's less chance of ugly mould forming. Always switch off the fan and turn the electricity off at the mains before cleaning. Remove the outer cover and wash in warm water and detergent. Wipe the blades (don't get them wet) with a damp cloth. Dry and replace.

229 TEA-TREE OIL TRICK

Try a natural disinfectant and deodorizer that's also effective as a fungicide. Place 2 teaspoons tea-tree oil and 2 cups of water in a spray bottle and spritz this around your bathroom to tackle mould and mildew.

230 WATCH FOR MOULD

Wood surrounds that are warping, cracked and peeling paintwork and stains on walls or ceilings are all signs of mould growth. Install fans that vent humidity to the outside and ensure your tumble dryer is venting air to the outside and not recirculating it within a room.

231 CERAMIC CARE

Wipe regularly with a damp sponge – add a splash of vinegar to the water or use commercial cleaner. Avoid soapy or oily cleaners and never use abrasives – these dull the finish and make glazed tiles more prone to dirt.

232 GROUT-BUSTER

Rid grout of mould and mildew by soaking paper towels in bleach and placing them around the grout (make sure you wear protective gloves for this and open the window first). Leave for at least an hour if not more. Remove the towels and enjoy clean white grout.

233 TLC FOR WOOD

Don't allow wooden surrounds or floors to become too wet. Wipe splashes at once. Avoid build-up on polished wood by wiping with a cloth dipped in water and vinegar, apply new polish sparingly and buff up in between. Liquid wax polish is easier to apply than solid wax and also helps remove dirt.

234 AVOID ACIDS

Natural acids such as lemon, vinegar and many bathroom cleansers can eat into marble, so keep these items well away from marble surfaces. Alcohol in perfumes, colognes and face treatments can also cause permanent etching.

235 CUT DOWN ON CLEANING

Apply mineral oil all over shower doors and tiled surfaces. This delays mineral build-up and cuts down on cleaning time.

236 MARBLE MAGIC

Marble is an excellent easy-care choice in bathrooms – it simply needs washing with a dishwashing liquid and warm water. Be sure to rinse thoroughly however, as a build-up could damage the stone. Always buff with a soft cloth until completely dry.

237 CITRUS CLEANER

Clean ceramic tiles the green way by wiping them with the cut side of a lemon. Leave for 15 minutes then polish up with a soft, dry cloth.

238 MOULD & MILDEW

Moisten a cloth or an old toothbrush with vinegar. Scrub away at the tile grout to remove mildew and mould; this also prevents new growth. Or use a disinfectant solution. Avoid abrasive steel wool.

239 WAX IT ON

Keep your shower tiles cleaner for longer by waxing with car polish after you clean to stop grease and grime sticking to them.

240 BEAT BLACK STAINS

Lick tough, black stains caused by damp with a paste made from borax and lemon juice or vinegar. Leave for half an hour, then scrub and rinse away.

toilets

241 START HERE

When cleaning the bathroom it makes good hygienic sense to clean the toilet first. Begin by placing disinfectant or diluted tea-tree oil in the toilet (this also keeps toilet brushes clean). Let it soak while you clean other bathroom areas.

242 COLA CLEANER

Toilet bowls come up shiny when cleaned with old flat cola. Pour a can into the bowl then leave at least an hour and flush – lime-scale dissolves easily.

243 DESTAIN YOUR LAVATORY

To prolong cleaning effects and to avoid nasty black streaks appearing in the toilet bowl, leave half a cup of vinegar in the lavatory overnight.

244 GRANDMA'S SECRET

Freshen up a grimy toilet bowl by adding two denture tablets. Leave overnight then flush for a lavatory that sparkles.

245 BOWL BRIGHTENER

Use all-purpose cleaner or sprinkle borax or baking soda in the bowl. Dampen with a little water to make a paste. Scrub with a toilet brush. Alternatively, make a paste from lemon juice and borax. Leave for two hours then scrub thoroughly.

246 CLEAN SWEEP

When it comes to cleaning the loo, good hygiene is essential. Wear rubber gloves always and make sure you use separate cloths (not sponges) to clean here. Soak them in a mix of bleach and water after use, or throw them away altogether.

247 DON'T MIX THEM UP!

Never use two different lavatory cleaners at the same time – they may combine to produce explosive or toxic gases. If you want to go green, use vinegar to clean your loo and its surrounds.

248 DAILY FRESHNESS

To avoid build-up, each day clean the inside of your toilet bowl and rim with a brush and proprietary cleaner. Alternatively, suspend a small block containing sanitizer, detergent and a light perfume under the rim of the bowl. Each time you flush, cleaner is released.

249 BATHROOM SPRITZ

Make your own air freshener by filling a spray bottle with about 100 ml (3 ½ fl oz) water and 10 drops of neroli oil which is renowned for its warm and relaxing qualities.

250 CLEAR THE AIR

To remove nasty whiffs in bathrooms, strike a match and blow it out – the sulphur will clear the air. Strategically place an air freshener close to the toilet, too.

251 PERFECT POTPOURRI

Make your own potpourri from mixed herbs such as peppermint and cloves, or sprinkle baking soda into a small basket or bowl to absorb smells in the bathroom.

252 PUMICED PERFECTION

Treat hard-to-shift rings round vitreous china bowls with a pumice stone (from drug stores). Wet the stone and rub away at the ring until it's gone. Avoid using pumice on enamel, plastic, fibreglass or other surfaces.

253 ROYAL FLUSH

To quickly freshen up your toilet, drop in two Alka Seltzer tablets, wait 20 minutes and then brush (avoid brushes with wire, which may scratch). Flush with the lid down to avoid a fine spray all over the bathroom.

254 SAVE WATER

Consider installing a water-saving toilet or fitting crystals in your cistern to save up to a litre per flush (from eco-friendly manufacturers). Certain crystals can save up to three litres a flush (around 5,000 litres (1,321 gallons) of water per person per year).

towels & accessories

255 BE KIND TO YOUR SKIN

Choose a mild detergent to wash towels – it's gentler on your skin and won't leave an artificial smell.

256 PILE 'EM HIGH

Bath sheets and small hand towels neatly folded on an open shelf lend a cosy feel to your bathroom.

257 TOWEL TALK

Between uses dry towels thoroughly. If you have space – and it's a sunny day – hang outside on a line to dry. Snip away pulled threads as soon as they appear and make sure everyone in the house has their own towel for hygienic and health sense.

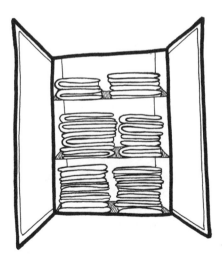

258 MIRROR MIRACLE

Make up a solution of equal parts of vinegar and water. Wearing rubber gloves use old newspapers to wipe the surface of the mirror with the mix. Add extra shine by rubbing with a clean blackboard eraser. Air freshener also works well and leaves a lovely fragrance.

WATER

vinegar

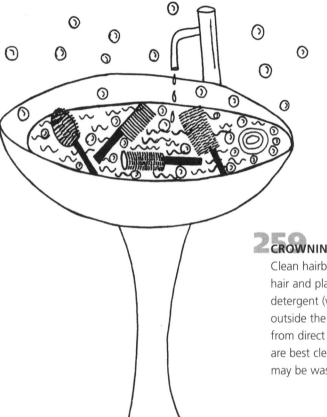

259 CROWNING GLORY

Clean hairbrushes regularly. Remove excess hair and place in a warm solution of diluted detergent (wooden handles should be left outside the water). Rinse well and dry away from direct heat. Tortoiseshell or bone combs are best cleaned with brushes. Plastic combs may be washed in warm soapy water.

260 COLOUR CARE

Wash sets of coloured towels at the same time so they fade equally. If towels fade dramatically, return them to the store where you bought them as it is possible they may be faulty. Use fabric softener just occasionally – too often and it will coat the towel, making it less absorbent.

261 TYPES OF TOWEL

Keep a selection of towels – bath sheets, bath towels, hand towels, guest towels and face cloths. You may find bath towels more practical than bath sheets, which are often bulky and hard to store. Towels with silk finishes can be less absorbent and detailing tricky to launder.

262 MARVELLOUS MATTING

Wash plastic mats in warm detergent solution. Cork and wooden slatted mats can be wiped with a clean cloth. Make sure your mat is machine-washed at least once a week and hang over the side of the bath or a heated towel rail in between to dry out thoroughly.

263 HOLLYWOOD LIGHTS

Install a mirrored cupboard above your sink to create extra storage space. Illuminated versions, like those found in hotel rooms, are perfect for plucking eyebrows.

264 KEEP IT FRESH

Rinse sponges and flannels thoroughly after use – hang up to dry and also to air. Every so often put them through a machine wash and hang out to dry. Sea sponges may be washed in warm soapy water.

265 STORAGE SPACES

If storage in your bathroom is limited, consider placing high-level shelves or cupboards on the upper half of the walls so the floor space is kept clear.

266 DEEP-PILE DECADENCE

Add a touch of luxury with a good supply of big, fluffy towels. The best ones have a deep pile and are more absorbent, making them more efficient. Install a heated towel rail to keep them dry and warm – the room will feel cosier, too.

267 BRUSH-OFF

To clean cosmetic brushes mix together two parts water with one part of gentle fabric wash but don't dip handles into the solution or they will become damaged.

268 GET RID OF GOO

Avoid slimy soap dishes by soaking them in 125 g (4 oz) washing soda crystals dissolved in 3½ litres (6 pints) of very hot water. Scrub with a nailbrush, rinse and dry.

269 WATCH FOR FLUFF

Put new towels through a wash according to the care label prior to use. Wash only similar shades together or the dyes could run. New towels often shred fluff so you may need to wash them separately for a few times before mixing loads.

270 STREAK-FREE MIRRORS

Instead of expensive glass cleaner, use a solution of ammonia and water to clean mirrors and glass shelving. The chemical mix of ammonia and water reduces streaking. Finish by wiping the surface with old newspapers.

271 MISTY MIRRORS

Reduce misting in bathrooms and kitchens by wiping mirrors with neat washing-up liquid. Buff up vigorously with kitchen paper. Or use an anti-mist product (from car and car accessory stores).

272 MEDICINE CUPBOARD

Choose a lockable cupboard to keep
dangerous medicines out of the reach of
children. Note that improperly sealed items can
evaporate leaving them more concentrated.

273 GET SOME THERAPY

Stock your shelves with several essential
oils. Five to 10 drops of organic essential
oil can be added to a running bath water:
camomile encourages a good night's sleep
while jasmine is invigorating and ginger can
help colds and flu.

bedding & linen

274 CLEANING DUVETS

Duvets with synthetic fillings can be washed in the bath according to the manufacturer's directions. Hang supported from two lines to ensure they dry in shape. Feather and down quilts should always be professionally cleaned.

275 BEST BUY

A duvet at least a size bigger than your bed will make your boudoir more extravagant and it will feel much cosier when you're tucked up inside it.

276 HEIRLOOM LACE

Visit markets to find antique linen and lace sheets and pillowcases. Wash by hand in the bath in warm water with a detergent designed for delicates. Rinse with warm water, do not wring, and dry flat.

277 PILE IT ON

You can dry-clean blankets but air well before using them again. Bring up the pile with a soft brush or shake well.

278 INSTANT MAKEOVER

Brighten up your bedroom with pretty linens. Try stripes and florals of the same hue or restrict the look to pure white for a calming effect.

279 LUSH LAUNDRY

Launder your bedding weekly in hot water to reduce dust and kill mites. Dry outdoors on a line if you can – it smells so much sweeter. An electric blanket keeps the bed dry and deters mites and mould at the same time.

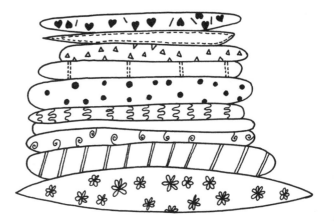

280 MARRIAGE GUIDANCE

If your partner has a habit of stealing most of the duvet, buy a French-style duvet cover with a flap at the bottom that tucks under the mattress, restricting duvet-hogging behaviour. Alternatively, make the bed with a top sheet beneath the duvet to prevent either one of you dragging the duvet over to your side.

281 BLANKET INSTRUCTION

Every three years clean and have electric blankets serviced by the manufacturers, who may also offer cleaning services. Often, the type of blankets with detachable control panels are washable. Spot-clean with a little washing-up liquid and water on a sponge; avoid over-wetting and dry naturally.

282 QUILT & DUVET CARE

New quilts can almost always be machine-washed (follow the care label instructions) but old or handmade ones need special care and should be professionally dry-cleaned. Both types are best aired afterwards outdoors on a clothesline if possible.

283 SAFETY FIRST

Discard any electric blanket that becomes frayed or if you discover scorch marks. Never use while damp. Examine the wiring inside often – hold the blanket up to the light to ensure no wires are overlapping, check the flex and the connections, too. Make sure your blanket lies flat on the bed. Store flat under the mattress or on a spare bed or roll – don't fold – if space is limited.

284 TALC TRICK

Freshen up blankets (including electric ones) by sprinkling them with a little talcum powder. Brush away the excess with a clothes brush.

285 SHEETS OF SATIN

Hand-wash acetate or silk satin sheets in lukewarm water using a gentle fabric wash. Hand-wring carefully – satin tears easily – in an absorbent white towel and hang to dry (this method also reduces pilling on polyester and nylon). Tumble-dry on the lowest setting. Never sun-dry satin or woven acetate in the sun.

286 SLEEP LIKE A BABY

Keep dust mites at bay by vacuuming your baby's bedding frequently. Most bed linen for newborns can only be washed at 40 °C (104 °F) and this will not kill dust mites so place it (and other warm-wash fabric) in the freezer overnight first.

287 THE WHITE STUFF

For the ultimate in luxury, buy white Egyptian cotton sheets. Be sure to choose a high thread count (400-plus). Launder only – do not wash at home – and watch the starch count. Good sheets will not pull into knotty fibres and last at least 10 years, if not a generation.

beds & futons

288 TIME FOR BED

To make a bed correctly, place the undersheet on top of the mattress with an even border all the way round and fold at the corners like a parcel, stretching the sheet as tightly as possible. Take the top two duvet corners and pull them inside the case. Slide in the bottom corners, secure and shake so the duvet is evenly distributed. Protect pillows with two pillowcases and plump them up perfectly to complete.

289 TOG TALK

Choose the right duvet for each season. Warmth is measuring in togs from 3 to 13.5. The lowest is a light summer weight (3–4.5); the highest 13.5 for the depths of winter. Consider a combination duvet – two buttoned together – to enjoy the best of both worlds.

290 MIXED BAG

Check the care label for the maximum temperature for cotton and polyester-cotton sheets and wash as a mixed load. Minimize ironing by removing still-damp sheets from the dryer; fold into eight and dry in an airing cupboard before ironing.

291 FENG SHUI FOR FUTONS

Choose a polyester-filled futon with a removable cover for washing or dry-cleaning (cotton and wool/cotton fillings are non-cleanable). Isolate any spills at once by tying with a rubber band then spot clean with water or mild detergent solution. Air regularly and turn weekly to prevent the mattress compacting.

292 HEAD START

Though pretty, fabric headboards also attract grease and dust. Vacuum your headboard often – whenever you clean the carpet. Remove marks with proprietary upholstery cleaner but be sure to open the windows first to air the room.

293 INVEST IN A DAY BED

If you live in a small space, perhaps a studio flat, consider buying an antique day bed. It will be a beautiful addition and, with pretty pillows strewn across it, will double up as extra seating during the day.

294 NEW MATTRESS

Buy a mattress with a water permeable (and washable) cover, which allows the fabric to breathe. Double-stitched seams last longer; check the zip is good quality, too. Help the filling to settle by turning the mattress over or around so head and foot are sometimes reversed.

295 TAKE A TURN

Did you know that the average bed has over 10,000 dust mites living in it? Turn your mattress every six months and vacuum both sides with the nozzle attachment. Protect with an underblanket or separate cover.

296 SPILT SOMETHING?

Tackle stains on mattresses with upholstery shampoo following the package directions. Dampen a sponge with warm water to apply the suds in a circular motion and draw moisture out with a clean dry towel. Leave as little water on the surface as possible to avoid mildew and mould growth.

297 SLAT CARE

Clean wooden slats or bed springs several times a year with a vacuum nozzle. Check the holding screws at the same time – they may need tightening to keep the base of the bed strong and supportive.

décor & ambience

298 GET TACTILE

Add a sensual feel to your bedroom with lots of contrasting textures for bedding, throws, carpets, curtains and upholstery. Try combining linen and cashmere with satin on a bedcover or cushions to achieve this.

299 DREAM ON

For deep and restful sleep, spritz pillowcases and sheets with lavender spray and drink camomile or other herb tea such as valerian (not caffeine) before you go to bed.

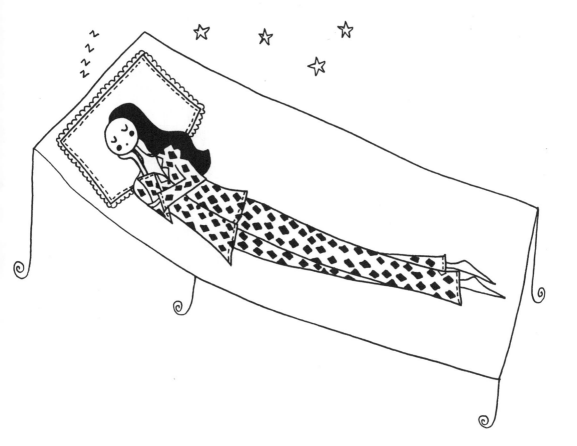

300 CLEAN AIR

Open windows, air blankets and your mattress by pulling down the covers and leaving them for an hour or so before making the bed again. Avoid hanging newly dry-cleaned clothes in the bedroom or using hairspray or other strong-smelling toiletries.

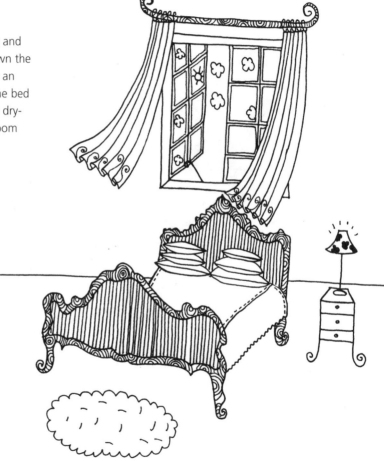

301 GIVE UP THE BOX

To encourage rest and sleep in your bedroom, consider moving out any TV or sound system. If you must have one in the bedroom, stick a piece of masking tape over the standby light, as studies have shown that even this small light can create a sleep disturbance.

302 WATCH THE LIGHTING

Gentle lighting encourages a restful mood. Avoid harsh overhead beams and instead install dimmer switches, soft uplighters and bedside lamps.

303 SCENTS FOR SLEEPING

Choose gentle and calming air fragrances or candles, such as lily of the valley, tuberose, orange blossom, honeysuckle or jasmine. For a good night's sleep, avoid heavily scented flowers in the bedroom.

304 INSTANT AMBIENCE

Spray a little perfume on a bedroom light bulb to create a lovely light scent in the room whenever the light is turned on.

305 COLOUR YOUR WORLD

Paint the walls of your bedroom in a single white or creamy shade but colour the wall behind your bed in a shade to match your mood. Experiment with colours you have never tried before or change seasonally.

306 HOME AWAY FROM HOME

To make travelling more comfortable, take a pashmina and a small pillow with you; also a set of mini scented candles. On arrival, throw the pashmina over your bed, add the pillow and light candles for instant ambience in a hotel room.

307 LIGHT REFLECTOR

A quick trick to make your bedroom appear bigger and brighter is to mount a mirror and mullion bars on a door to give the impression that it's a glass door without losing your privacy. The mirror will reflect the light and add space.

308 GO VERTICAL

Choose tall rather than wide furniture if you want your room to seem larger. Vertical lines draw the eye upwards and increase the feeling of space.

309 KEEP OUT CLUTTER

Make your bedroom your sanctuary by keeping clutter to a minimum. Avoid old newspapers or piles of anything that will make you feel hemmed in.

guest rooms

310 HANG IT ALL

Offer your guests plenty of hanging space (include a few covered hangers) and drawers to store their clothes away. Otherwise the room will feel cluttered and uncomfortable for the duration of their stay.

311 BEDTIME STORIES

Place two or three interesting books on the bedside table. Collections of short stories, a classic novel and perhaps a fun piece of chick-lit will be appreciated by guests, as will a magazine or two.

79

312 SNUGGLE UP

Extra blankets and throws look pretty on the end of a bed – your guests can use them if they get cold in the night, too.

313 CREATURE COMFORTS

Leave a spare dressing gown, plenty of fluffy towels and some glamorous soap in your guestroom. A small bowl of fresh fruit or luxurious chocolates adds a welcoming touch.

314 DECORATE WITH SCENT

Before friends or family arrive to stay, light a scented candle (do not leave it unattended) or spray the bed linen in their room to encourage relaxing sleep. Choose fragrances with spicy, citrus, fruity or floral notes, depending on your guests personality.

315 PERFECTLY SPACED

Make the guest bedroom as cosy and inviting as you can so your guests will want to spend time there. The pressure for both parties to constantly entertain one another will be removed, too.

jewellery

316 AMBER LIGHT

Wipe amber jewellery over with a soft cloth wrung out in warm soapy water. Dry at once (water makes amber cloudy). A wiping of sweet almond oil will remove grease marks.

317 CROWN JEWELS

Polish costume jewellery by dropping two Alka Seltzer tablets into a glass of water. Immerse for about five minutes and pat dry on kitchen paper.

318 GENTLY DOES IT

Occasionally wipe gold and platinum with the softest of clean chamois. Ordinary cloths may hold grit that could damage the surface. Gold plate should be treated with tender care or the thin layer may rub off with excessive polishing.

319 MAGNIFICENT MARCASITE

Bring back the magic of marcasite by polishing with a soft brush and then buff with a chamois – it should never be washed.

322 GIRL'S BEST FRIEND

Diamonds – and also amethysts, rubies and sapphires – can be cleaned in a solution of washing-up liquid. Scrub gently with a soft toothbrush. Rinse in lukewarm water and dip in surgical spirit to remove any remaining detergent film. Drain on paper towels and buff with a chamois. Never store diamonds together – although extremely hard, they could still scratch each other.

323 PURE & SIMPLE

Since turquoise and opals are porous stones, never immerse them in water. Instead polish with a soft, dry chamois and clean claws with a soft bristle brush.

324 PROTECTION RACKET

Remove silver rings when cooking, cleaning, washing-up and swimming; also avoid contact with food to protect silver from tarnishing. Clean with a proprietary silver polish specially designed for use on silver. Remove all traces of polish or this will cause tarnishing and also leave marks on clothing.

320 PROLONG PEARLS

The best way to care for a pearl (or coral) necklace is to wear it regularly – oils in your skin add a gentle lustre. After wearing, wipe with a chamois to remove traces of perspiration that can damage the surface. Wash in water and very mild soap then wipe with a soft cloth. Lay on moist kitchen paper to dry.

321 PRECIOUS & SEMI-PRECIOUS

Gentle detergent and water plus a soft cloth will clean rubies, amethysts, citrines, sapphires, turquoise and garnets.

325 SOFT TOUCH

Emeralds are softer than other precious stones and can chip easily. Wash carefully in a warm solution of washing-up liquid.

pillows

326 FORGET THE LAUNDRETTE

Often it's best to have pillows professionally cleaned – if you do them yourself they can become lumpy and hard. Never use the dry-cleaning machine at the laundrette: the chemical fumes are difficult to remove. But if you want to clean them at home, see the tips below.

327 WATCH THE WEIGHT

Before machine-washing pillows, check the manufacturer's instruction for your machine – there may be a limit to the amount of weight it can take. Some natural fillings can become heavy when soaked in water. If in doubt, have them professionally cleaned.

328 NIGHTS IN WHITE SATIN

Clean satin pillows in all shades with the soft brush attachment of the vacuum cleaner. Treat greasy stains to a sprinkling of flour or talcum powder, leave overnight and brush off the excess. If stains are stubborn, launder only if the pillow has a removable cover.

329 PILLOW TALK

Have plenty of pillows so you literally sink into your bed. Avoid washing feather pillows as this removes the natural oils – dry-clean and air thoroughly to get rid of solvent fumes. Polyester can be washed according to the care label: do not dry-clean or tumble-dry.

330 PLUMP UP PILLOWS

To restore fluffiness to bed pillows, simply place them in your tumble-dryer for a few minutes – the warm air works wonders. Frequent laundering will reduce the life of a pillow so this is a great way to bring back the bounce for 10 minutes twice a year between washes.

331 FRESHEN UP FOAM

Once a year, sponge foam pillows in warm soapy water. Rinse well – remove excess water by wrapping in an absorbent towel: do not wring. Dry away from sunlight and direct heat.

shoes & accessories

332 BUFFED-UP BRILLIANCE

Remove surface dirt from leather shoes and boots with a soft brush. Leave mud to dry and then remove with a stiff brush followed by a soft damp cloth. Apply polish or shoe cream with a soft brush or cloth. Brush with a medium brush and buff to a high shine.

333 SAVE YOUR SHOES

Avoid wearing shoes and boots every day or they quickly lose their shape and look tired. Use wooden trees to keep them in good shape and have them repaired regularly. Extend the life of evening shoes by filling them with tissue after wear.

334 SCENTED SACHETS

If your shoes are a little smelly place a sheet of fabric softener in them overnight. Or create a sachet by placing two or three teaspoons of bicarbonate of soda in the middle of a circle of cotton. Secure with a rubber band and place a sachet in each shoe overnight.

335 TACKLING TRAINERS

Rinse trainers (and other fabric shoes) in clear water and scrub with a soft cloth and non-scented hand wash. Scour scuffs with a white, nylon-backed scrubbing pad. Rinse and air-dry. Or squirt on foam shaving cream – leave for half an hour and brush off the excess then wipe with a damp cloth. To retain the shape, stuff with white paper.

336 TAKE A SPIN

If suitable, spray canvas and synthetic shoes – especially when grass stained – with stain removal spray. Wipe and place in a mesh bag for a regular wash. Add light-coloured towels to the machine – the rubbing action helps clean the trainers and prevents them from bouncing around too much and damaging your machine.

337 PICTURE PERFECT

To access shoes more easily, take a Polaroid of each pair and glue to the front of shoe-boxes, or buy storage boxes in clear or frosted plastic. Vintage or delicate clothes can also be given the Polaroid treatment and packed away in tissue and cardboard boxes.

338 PATENTLY SO

Clean patent leather with a soft cloth wrung out in diluted detergent and buff with a soft dry cloth. Wax cracks leather so wipe a little milk over the surface and then buff for still more shine.

339 SWEETEN UP SUEDE

Brush suede shoes with a special bristle or wire brush in a circular motion but be gentle or you will damage the delicate surface of the fabric.

340 TREAT YOUR TRAINERS

Buff up your leather trainers with a soft cloth and leather cleaner and conditioner. Avoid machine-washing as this can damage the shape.

341 TRY A LITTLE TLC

Store your handbags stuffed with crumpled tissue paper to retain their shape – delicate evening bags are often supplied with a protective cover. Any repairs should be handed over to a specialist – especially if the bag happens to be your best Birkin.

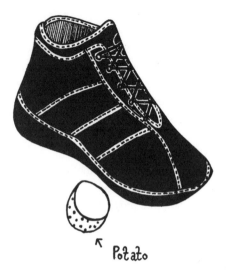

↖ Potato

342 HAPPY FEET

Soften leather shoes by rubbing with lemon or castor oil. Help prevent cracking and drying by wiping with olive oil. To wear in new shoes, rub alcohol in at the heels and wear while still-wet. Potato peelings will soften shoes if left in overnight. Treat scuffs by wiping them with the cut edge of a raw potato and then buff with a cloth afterwards.

343 CAR WASH

Try a plastic cleaner sold in car supply stores on plastic, vinyl or polyurethane bags. You can also use baby wipes. Spray with silicone wax spray after cleaning and then buff to restore the shine.

344 FABRIC FRESHENERS

Add half a teaspoon of gentle fabric wash to 60 ml (2 fl oz) lukewarm water for all-over cleaning of sturdy fabrics. Apply neat to spots and stains. Barely-damp baby wipes will work on delicate fabric bags.

345 PATENT PERFECTION

Real patent can be cleaned with cream cleaner conditioner but be gentle: it scratches easily. On imitation leather, use washing-up liquid.

346 SADDLE UP

Use saddle soap or cream leather cleaner on real leather according to the manufacturer's directions. Follow up with solvent-free conditioner to avoid drying out and buff with a soft cloth.

347 A HEAD FOR HATS

Keep hats in good shape by vacuuming them every so often. Hats have a tendency to attract dust, so use the upholstery tool on a low suction but protect trimmings with a cloth. If you have several hats in your wardrobe and enough space, buy attractive hat-boxes to store them.

348 SQUASHED STRAW

Rescue a straw hat by placing a damp cloth between the straw and a fairly hot iron (don't let it sit on the straw). Rest the brim underside up on the ironing board and press rotating the hat as you go. For flat tops, place cardboard inside and pack with crumpled newspaper before pressing. A pudding basin is a better base for a round crown. Finish with a dry iron but avoid direct contact.

349 SHORT STRAW

Clean natural straw bags with a solution of one part liquid hand soap to three parts water. Air-dry on a clothes rack.

352 FABRIC SOLUTIONS

To clean fabric or woven belts, place a towel on top of a work surface and the belt on top. Now mix 50 ml (1¾ fl oz) gentle fabric cleaner with 1 litre (1¾ pints) water. Dampen a small area with a cloth to check for colourfastness. Dab the surface with solution, one section at a time. Rinse and blot with water then towel-dry. Buff metal buckles with a cloth.

wardrobes

350 SPRUCE UP SUEDE

Brush the nap with a natural bristle shoe brush to remove surface dirt or have suede professionally cleaned. Use protector sprays sparingly: some attract dirt. Apply talcum powder to grease marks and leave overnight to absorb the stain then brush.

351 LEATHER LIFESAVER

Prolong the life of leather belts with leather protector (without wax or silicone). Clean dirty belts and remove stains with a damp cloth or sponge dabbed in saddle soap. Wipe away the excess and buff with a dry cloth.

353 AVOID CRUSHES

Make sure there's enough space for clothes to hang freely or you will end up ironing them twice. If you have an extensive range, consider buying a second wardrobe, wall-to-wall cupboards or creating a dressing room out of a box room.

354 KEEP TIES CREASE-FREE

Store ties in a special tie holder inside the wardrobe so you can easily select one and avoid creases.

355 GROUP GARMENTS

To save time, arrange clothes according to type – trousers, skirts, dresses and coats/jackets – and by colour.

356 BUTTON CARE

Wooden buttons may be cleaned with wood oil cleanser and residue removed with a soap cloth. Use saddle soap to condition leather buttons (remove from the garment first). Metal buttons respond well to an application of non-gel toothpaste: buff well afterwards.

357 WOOLLEN WONDER

Instead of taking a woollen coat, dress or skirt to the dry cleaner, lay it out on a table and sprinkle a thin, even layer of salt on top. Make a pad from a piece of folded linen and use this to rub the salt gently into the cloth with long sweeping movements (circular ones will roughen the surface). Place the garment on a hanger and brush vigorously with a stiff clothes brush. Repeat on cuffs, collars and hems as necessary.

358 EDIT ITEMS

Every season set aside an afternoon or even a whole day to simplify your wardrobe. Decide what you really need and what is taking up precious space. Sell on e-Bay (especially designer clothes and accessories), recycle or give unwanted clothes away to charity. Clean, repair and pack up anything you don't need. Replace lavender bags and moth repellents at the same time.

359 GET FRESH

To keep wardrobes smelling sweet, air coats and jackets before putting them back, especially if you've been out on the town. Add cedar to your wardrobe – it smells delicious and also wards off moths.

360 FACELIFT FOR LEATHER

Give a leather jacket a new lease of life by covering it with a paste of fine white pure clay and water. Add just enough water for a spreading consistency. Work from the bottom of the garment to the top, rubbing it in. Leave to dry and then shake until all the clay has dropped off.

361 STOW AWAY

Attractive storage units under the bed are good out-of-the-way places to keep off-season clothes, shoes or accessories. If you choose free-standing units, make sure they have lids to keep off the dust and are exactly the same style to achieve a co-ordinated effect. Do not neglect dusting under the bed as a result – you will need to clean even more.

362 KEEP IN SHAPE

Retain the shape of clothes by leaving tailor's stitches in new jackets and coats. This will prevent you filling the pockets or putting your hands inside while wearing them. Any pockets should be emptied before you return clothes to the closet.

363 SPACE SOLUTIONS

Create extra storage by using the space under your bed. Keep items in boxes, baskets or purpose made under-bed storage – the best are fitted with castors so everything is accessible and you can clean under the bed easily.

364 ROUTINE CLEAN

Depending on how often you wear them, take ties to a professional cleaner once or twice a year. Look for a company experienced in cleaning silk ties and ask how they finish the tie (rolled and reshaped with steam, not pressed is best). Don't hand your best ties over to a new cleaner until you're sure they can handle them.

365 PERFECT VINTAGE

Avoid snagging delicate vintage clothes by hanging them carefully, or even placing them in tissue-filled boxes. Any 'new' vintage clothes should be professionally cleaned before they enter your wardrobe or they could destroy your other clothes with moth larvae.

366 HERE COMES SUMMER

Wash and dry winter clothes. Place them in zip-up plastic bags that can be stored under the bed. Prevent moths from attacking them by using the nozzle of a vacuum cleaner to suck out air at the opening of the bags so they are vacuum-packed.

367 ORGANIZED STYLE

Display handbags and accessories on hooks clustered together inside a closet door or on one wall of a walk-in wardrobe for a pretty feature. Be sure to dust them regularly.

368 WELL-SUPPORTED

Throw away wire hangers from dry-cleaners or you will end up with shapeless, crushed clothes. If you've broken the budget barrier and bought yourself a little designer number, invest in a decent hanger – compared to the garment, the cost will seem small.

369 TREAT TIES TENDERLY

Never try to remove a stain on a tie with water or you may create a large watermark that's hard to remove. Blot away excess stains (salad dressing, sauces and gravy are popular ones) with a napkin or clean white cloth. Take to the dry cleaner as soon as possible: stains set after 24 or 48 hours. Don't attempt to rub the stain out or you could rub colour from the fabric, especially if silk.

370 MIRROR, MIRROR

Invest in a full-length mirror. If space in the bedroom is limited, fix one to the back of a wardrobe door. You'll be able to see whether your outfit works and check for dropped hems or stains instantly.

FLAT LINERS

Line drawers with scented drawer-liners,
gift-wrap or brown paper and spray with
essential oils. You can also add bunches of
lavender or used perfume bottles or testers
from cosmetic counters without the lids.
Scented sachets look sweet
among lingerie.

372 SMART STORAGE

Antique chests or luggage trunks can hide away spare sheets, pillows and pillowcases, duvets and blankets when not in use. Tie sets of bedding together with pretty ribbon or tape so you can access them easily.

373 STAY SILKY

If your outfit is made of silk, apply hair spray and make-up before getting dressed if possible. Both contain alcohol that could cause the dyes in the silk to bleed.

374 CLOTHES HORSE

A hanging rail is a good solution if you have an extensive collection of clothes. It's also a cheap alternative to a wardrobe. Keep clothes dust-free by covering them in an attractive sheet.

375 LUGGAGE CARE

Brush suede luggage with a special suede brush and keep leather supple with wax polish. The best way to treat patent leather is to smear it with petroleum jelly then buff dry.

376 DRAWER FRESHENERS

Wash wooden drawers in warm soapy water. For laminated plastic, use 25 ml (1 fl oz) white vinegar mixed with 1 litre (1¾ pints) of warm water. Air-dry if possible or wipe with paper towels.

377 TRUNK CALL

If a suitcase or trunk has a musty smell, place an open tin of clay cat litter inside. Close and leave overnight.

children's rooms

378 BANISH BABY STAINS

Fresh stains on upholstery from baby food and formula milk may be soaked in cold water for 30 minutes and then placed under cold running water. Gently rub the fabric together to loosen the stain and launder in the machine on a warm wash. Old or dried-on stains may require liquid detergent or even oxygen bleach (follow the manufacturer's instructions).

379 BREAD LINE

Although it sounds obvious, most pencil marks can be removed with a white eraser but treat painted walls and fabrics gently. Alternatively press a piece of fresh bread into a wall stain to extract it.

380 BRILLIANT BORAX

When the kids have sprinkled their supper all over the carpet, remove the excess and dampen the carpet with water. Sprinkle borax (a natural, eco-friendly salt) over the surface and leave according to the manufacturer's instructions. Vacuum later.

381 CRAYON CREATIVES

When it comes to crayoning, kids will always be attracted to the walls of your home. Marks on painted walls, glass, metal, tiles, marble or porcelain may be sprayed with a penetrating lubricant and then wiped with a soft cloth. Wipe persistent waxy marks in a circular motion.

382 CAT LITTER CLEANSER

To remove fresh vomit from a hard surface, pour cat litter into it to absorb it. Sweep up and wipe the surface with a damp sponge. Lift solids from carpets with paper towels and sponge with cool water. Sprinkle with bicarbonate of soda and dry. Vacuum and sponge with a solution of washing-up liquid. Rinse and blot dry.

383 GOOD EXAMPLE

Get kids into the habit of clearing up at the end of the day before they go to bed. Toys and games can be stashed away in trunks and have plenty of novelty hooks to hang schoolbags and sports equipment.

384 ICE & EASY

Use ice cubes to freeze chewing gum left on a chair. Scrape away the surface with a knife and repeat as necessary.

385 OUT, DAMNED SPOT

Remove washable ink stains with cool water (or soda water while wet) but permanent pen and Biro requires methylated spirit. Allow at least 30 minutes for the stain to dissolve. Or apply alcohol to the stain with a clean white cloth towel and blot later with a fresh white towel.

386 PRISTINE PRAMS

Clean buggies and prams with a sprinkling of baking soda on a damp paper towel. Wipe down and rinse with warm water. More persistent marks can be removed with the suds (not water) from a solution of washing-up liquid.

387 TOY STORY

Blot juice and other spills on stuffed toys with kitchen paper. Wet with a cloth or sponge and blot again. Repeat until the stain is gone. Machine-wash according to the care label in a pillowcase or hand wash in warm soapy water. Air-dry and preen with a hairbrush.

cleaning surfaces

388 DUST-BUSTERS

Anti-bacterial wipes with natural citrus extract are a relatively recent invention. These scented sheets quickly pick up dust and kill off bacteria across the home leaving you free to do other things.

389 DUST TRAP

Wrap a paper towel around the broad end of a kitchen spatula and secure with a rubber band. Use this to reach dust trapped between tubes of a radiator. Spray the kitchen paper with all-purpose cleaner to get rid of sticky spills and stains.

390 HAVE A ROUTINE

To keep on top of dusting, at least once a week dust obvious areas such as tables and other exposed surfaces. If something is particularly dusty deal with it there and then. Dust tops of pictures, bookshelves, lampshades, lights, skirtings and sills monthly.

391 JUST DO IT!

Dust little and often and you'll prolong the life of your furniture and give your home a fresher appearance. Take care to remove dust properly – don't just move it around. Use a clean duster and shake it outside afterwards. Don't duck out of dusting around legs and feet of furniture. Avoid using a feather duster on valuable furniture: broken feathers may scratch the surface.

392 CLEAN HEAT

Dirty radiators are far less efficient than clean ones – because heat attracts dust, clean once a week. Hang a damp towel behind a radiator to remove dust and cobwebs. Blow from the front with the cylindrical attachment of a vacuum cleaner or hair dryer.

cushions & accessories

393 CHOOSE CAREFULLY

Ideally opt for cushions with removable covers and wash them often, according to the care label. Non-removable cushions may be cleaned with upholstery shampoo. Avoid washing feather-filled cushions (the feathers will poke out of the fabric); kapok too becomes lumpy over time so replace pads regularly.

394 BE GENTLE

Vacuum cushions with the nozzle part of the vacuum cleaner and not the whole attachment. Surface dirt is quickly removed and less suction means less risk of the cushions becoming ripped or damaged. Wash covers according to the care label.

395 IMPROVE AIR QUALITY

Keep cushions fresh and avoid dust-stains by vacuuming them at least once a month. You'll also avoid dust mites that can trigger off all kinds of allergies.

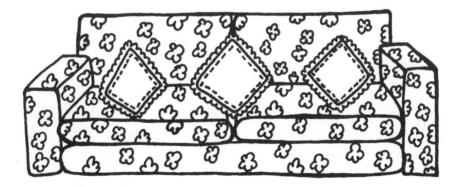

396 SILK SAFETY

Handwash cushion covers and other small items made of silk in hand-hot water and soapflakes. To avoid weakening the fibres soak for just a few minutes and dry out of the sun to prevent the colours from fading. Reverse iron while damp on a cool temperature. Take larger items such as curtains to a specialist dry-cleaner.

397 BRUSH OFF

Remove dust from books with a clean, soft, slightly damp paintbrush or make-up brush. Take each book individually off the shelf; dust outwards from the binding. It's fine to flip the pages to dust them – just don't bang them together.

398 SADDLE SOLUTION

Leather bindings respond well to a light application of saddle soap (be careful not to touch the paper or cloth parts of the book). Massage in gently until the soap has been absorbed. The leather will almost certainly be darkened but in centrally heated homes this prevents it from drying out.

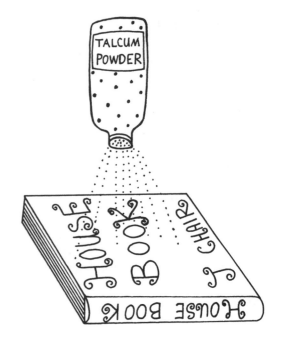

399 MAGIC AWAY MILDEW

Dust mildewed pages with cornflour, French chalk or talcum powder. Leave inside the closed book for several days then brush it off.

400 GREASE ELIMINATOR

Place a piece of blotting paper on either side of a page with grease spots. Press gently with a warm iron to remove.

401 HANDLE WITH CARE

Valuable antique books should always be cleaned and restored by a professional, who will also be able to advise on their maintenance.

402 HAVE A HUMIDIFIER

Central heating damages backings and bindings so keep a humidifier in a room where books are displayed. Or add a bowl of water to provide a little moisture in the atmosphere.

403 WAX WONDER

If your candelabra is coated in wax – and especially if it's made of glass – place in the freezer for an hour. You'll find the wax will chip off more easily.

404 STRAIGHTEN UP

When a picture refuses to hang straight, wrap clear adhesive tape around the centre of the wire to prevent it from slipping sideways.

405 CLEAR VISION

Mirrors and glass frames may be cleaned with a cloth wrung out in water to which a little vinegar has been added. Polish with paper towels or a chamois. Fly spots will respond well to a coating of cold tea, while wooden frames can be brought to life with a little olive oil.

406 FIT A FRAME

Framing helps photos to last longer but avoid hanging framed photos or pictures in direct sunlight or they will fade. Wipe away dust with glass cleaner and a soft cloth. Never spray directly onto the glass: cleaning solution could drip behind the frame and damage precious photos.

407 SAFE STORAGE

Negatives and old prints should be stored out of sunlight in an even temperature. Place in polyester covers to prevent them sticking together or colours becoming bleached. A cool dry place is best for keeping albums and boxes of photos – under the bed is ideal.

408 PERFECT CONDITIONS

Never hang a valuable, original piece of art over a radiator or fireplace – the heat will damage it. Also avoid damp walls and direct sunlight. Spray cleaning fluid onto the glass, not the picture, or it could seep through and damage both frame and masterpiece.

409 INHERITED A MASTERPIECE?

Avoid tampering with a painting that might be valuable. Cleaning and restoration is best left to professionals. Your local art dealer or art store may be able to offer advice.

410 PHOTO FINISH

Photos last longer if you look after them properly. Store in good-quality paper albums interleaved with acid-free paper. Secure in position with special photo corners rather than glue.

décor & design

411 PARE DOWN

Avoid surrounding yourself with more possessions or furniture than you really have room for. Anything unused for six months will probably never be used so throw it out or give it away. If you don't have time to dust often, limit ornaments and avoid open shelving which looks fantastic but needs regular upkeep.

412 LET YOUR LOOK EVOLVE

It takes time to create a room that's full of character so don't rush it. If funds are limited, save up to buy one or two really beautiful pieces of furniture or an amazing picture rather than items you'll just want to replace at a later date. Less really is more.

413 PERFECTLY SPACED

Avoid making a feature out of woodwork. Instead contrast tones with the walls. In small rooms, paint floors the same colour as the walls to extend the illusion of space. White painted floorboards give any room an instant lift.

414 STRIKE A BALANCE

On walls keep a neutral palette and introduce colour through accessories and upholstery so you can follow fashion and easily alter the look of your room according to the season with cushions, throws and other touches. Powerful statements in every room are often hard to live with.

415 PLAN AHEAD

Consider how you want to use your living room – whether you need space to entertain, study, read and so on. This makes arranging furniture so much easier.

416 MAKE A STORYBOARD

Buy a notice board and pin to it all the ideas and colour schemes you have for a room. You may not be able to do everything at once but you'll be able to see how your look comes together and you also have time to change your mind as you build your room.

417 CLEAN & CLEAR FIRST

For a quick transformation in any room, start with a thorough clean and a few subtle changes. Try moving the furniture around, paint one wall in a cool colour, add pictures or different cushion covers or throws.

418 SHELVE IT

Have plenty of shelves and extra surfaces to hold books and ornaments to avoid filling up valuable floor space and making a room feel cluttered.

418 UNDERCOVER SECRETS

Stylish baskets and boxes are the perfect solution for stashing away newspapers, CDs and toys whenever you need to do a quick tidy-up. Cupboards and antique chests, too, create an atmosphere of calm and will hold an enormous amount of things.

420 DIVIDE & RULE

Make your rooms multipurpose. Separate work-live spaces with a clever use of screens. Or create a dining area by running open bookshelves across one part of the room.

entertaining

421 BRING OUT THE BUBBLY

Place champagne in the bottom of the fridge the day before a celebration so that it's chilled perfectly. Though it may sound obvious, check the direction the bottle is pointing in before you open it. For more control, turn the bottle with one hand and keep your other hand at the top with your fingers over the cork.

422 COCKTAIL HOUR

Always use well-chilled glasses for cocktails. If there's not enough room in the fridge or freezer to chill them for a few minutes, leave to stand with ice inside. Gin and vodka will not freeze so can be stored in the freezer.

424 WAX WONDER

To remove candle wax from a table or cloth, place some brown paper (not newspaper) over the top and iron it on a low heat. Avoid coloured candles on white cloths: the dye is difficult to remove.

423 BEST BARTENDER

When entertaining, have lots of ice in the freezer and plenty of glasses. Buy bags of crushed ice and hire glasses from your local store. Stock up with soft drinks as well as alcohol. Or opt for vodka-based cocktails which won't stain carpets.

425 WALLFLOWER WATCH

Avoid leaving a single chair on its own or a shy person will end up sitting there with no one to talk to. Place one or two small tables beside sofas and chairs so there's plenty of space to put down drinks and nibbles.

426 DAISY CHAIN

Get together a group where everyone knows someone but no one knows everyone. Be brave: ask new people and keep to a number that fits comfortably round your table. For larger parties, invite more than you expect – people always drop out at the last minute but give close friends plenty of notice.

427 FINISHING TOUCHES

On the day of your party, go to a flower market and buy bunches of flowers cheaply and in bulk. For extra impact, choose flowers and foliage of one kind and one colour. Arrange them casually in tall vases and carefully dot night-lights around for mood and atmosphere.

428 MUSIC MAESTRO

Have a mix of music – uplifting beats for when everyone arrives (but quiet enough so they can chat, too), dance music for when the party really gets going and ambient moods for late into the night (and to keep the neighbours happy).

429 PERFECT PLANNING

Before buying food for a dinner party, ring round to confirm the number of guests. Check if there are any vegetarians; also any dietary preferences.

430 MAKE A START

However late or tired you are at the end of the evening, empty ashtrays and remove bottles of wine, cutlery and glasses from the living room if you can. If you can't face washing up, pile it sensibly in the kitchen to avoid heightening a hangover the next day.

equipment

431 SMOOTH OUT SCRATCHES

Scratches in DVDs and CDs are in the surface coating of the disc, not in the data information so you can fill in the scratch with an optical material or polish it down with a commercial product or even a little toothpaste. Polish in straight lines away from the centre to avoid creating any new scratches.

432 CD & CASSETTE CARE

Store away from direct heat and sunlight in the cases provided. Hold by the edges and dust from the centre outwards with a soft clean cloth. Remove finger marks with a cloth dampened in mild detergent or try isopropyl alcohol (from chemists).

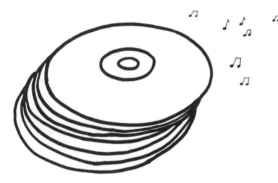

433 CHEAP & CHEERFUL

Make your own anti-static cloth. First, soak a lint-free cloth in fabric softener diluted in water. Squeeze out excess liquid and dry before use. Treat several cloths at the same time to ensure a good supply.

434 REVITALIZE VCRS & TAPES

Turn off your VCR and wipe the front, sides and top (away from vent holes) with a soft cotton cloth and glass cleaner sprayed directly onto the cloth, not the machine. Do the same with the cables. Dust around sensitive controls and the back with a small dry paintbrush.

435 DIRT CAN DAMAGE

Video cassettes, CDs and DVDs can be damaged by dirty drives so buy a cleaning cassette, or CD or DVD drive-cleaning disc from an electronics shop, or have your machine professionally cleaned. Store equipment in a cool, dry place and avoid sudden changes in temperature.

436 TAKE CARE

Always switch off and unplug appliances before cleaning them. Dust regularly with a soft cloth or feather duster. Reduce static by wiping over with a special cloth (see tip 433 above). Grease and other spots may be removed with a soft cloth dampened with methylated spirits.

437 REMOVE LABELS

Loose labels are one of the biggest causes of VCR jams so always remove them from video cassettes.

438 YOUR CALL

Telephones attract dust so wipe over regularly with a damp cloth coated in mild detergent. Dry with a soft, clean cloth. Disinfect with one of the antibacterial products now available or use mouthwash, especially if someone in your family has been ill. Place on a cloth and then wipe.

flowers & plants

439 HAPPY HOLIDAYS

Before going on vacation, place your plants in the bath with a little water. To maintain a moist atmosphere, cover the bath top with a polythene sheet, leaving a few gaps to allow air inside. Draw the curtains, too, if the sun is likely to shine directly on the plants.

440 CHOOSE LIFE

To prolong the life of cut flowers, add 2 tablespoons vinegar and 1 teaspoon sugar to the water. An aspirin or two in the water is also reputed to work. In both instances, change the water every few days.

441 SOUNDS FISHY

If you have an aquarium, save the water each time you change it and use it to water your houseplants. You'll be amazed at the results.

442 LONG-LASTING BLOOMS

To keep flowers fresh for as long as possible, change the water and trim the stems every day. Crush rose stems at the ends to encourage absorption of water. If you can't change the water every day, place a copper coin in with the flowers. Tulips last longer if you make a series of small holes with a pin down the length of their stems.

443 TOXIC TENDRILS

Don't add daffodils to a mixed vase of flowers – they produce a toxin that kills off the other flowers.

444 PINK SODA

Carnations and pinks last longer if you place them in carbonated lemonade (not the diet variety) rather than water. Change every four days.

445 REVITALIZE TIRED TENDRILS

To revive cut flowers, plunge the end of the stems into boiling water. By the time the water cools the flowers will have perked up perfectly. Trim the stems and place in fresh cold water.

446 LEAFY WONDERS

If the lower leaves of stems trail in water they will rot and the flowers won't last long so remove wilted blooms and leaves regularly. To keep vases free from slime and avoid stale smells, add just a few drops of bleach to the water – this will not harm the flowers.

447 DISAPPEARING ACT

Wash the inside of a vase with warm water and detergent. Neat vinegar removes green slime and watermarks. Leave inside for five or 10 minutes then clean with a brush. Rinse and dry.

448 GET ARTFUL WITH ARTIFICIAL

To revitalize artificial flowers, pour salt into a large paper bag. Place the flowers inside, heads down, and shake vigorously. The dirt will be transferred to the salt. Perk up paper flowers by applying a steam iron on the lowest setting.

449 RICE RINSE

Remove white deposits from the inside of cut-glass vases by filling the vase with malt vinegar and a handful of dry rice. Swirl the mixture around and leave overnight. Rinse in hot soapy water. Less-than-sweet vases will be freshened up too.

450 POLISH UP PLANTS

Bring up the shine on leafy indoor plants by polishing them with cotton wool soaked in olive oil or milk. To encourage growth, remove dead leaves and flowers and remember to turn them regularly as they will grow towards the light.

451 VASE BRIGHTENERS

Remove stubborn stains from the base of a glass vase by filling it with water and dropping in two Alka Seltzer tablets – this trick also works on glass cruets. Alternatively, swirl a mixture of vinegar and sea salt inside – salt gently scours the surface of the glass while the vinegar breaks down deposits.

452 PURE GENIUS

According to a two-year study by NASA, certain houseplants are not only beautiful but they also help cleanse the air by removing harmful pollutants. Try bamboo palm, spider plant, peace lily and English ivy.

furniture & furnishings

453 AVOID SILICONE & OIL

Silicone-based cleaning sprays leave a film on wood that's hard to remove while oil-based polishes attract dirt and some can even darken the wood. Instead use a natural polish such as beeswax.

454 CANE CARE

Regularly vacuum with the brush attachment of your cleaner. Dirtier cane can be washed with a solution of mild detergent (avoid harsh cleaners or detergents) and water applied with a cloth. Rinse in clear water and dry with a towel.

455 KEEP YOUR COOL

The temperature in your home hugely affects the condition of your furniture. If it's excessively dry, furniture will dry out and shrink while dampness can cause mould. Keep pieces in an even temperature and humidity.

456 BAMBOO & PAPER PIECES

Clean furniture made of these materials with a sponge dampened in soapy water (never hose). Wipe with a sponge moistened with clear water then wipe dry. Every so often apply a thin coat of liquid or paste wax to bamboo to keep it in good condition.

457 FANTASTIC PLASTIC

Wipe acrylics and plastics with a damp cloth and deal with dirty marks with a small amount of neat washing-up liquid. Never use scourers or harsh abrasives. Treat scratches on acrylics by rubbing in a small amount of non-gel toothpaste. Buff until both toothpaste and scratch have totally disappeared.

458 BUSY BEE

Protect the finish of wooden furniture by applying a good-quality beeswax polish at least once a year, twice if furniture is used heavily. Apply sparingly with a soft cloth and polish up with another lint-free cloth. Rub and rub again for a good shine rather than adding layer upon layer of wax.

459 CROWD PLEASER

Extend a wooden dining table by placing a large piece of sturdy plywood on top. Draw the outline of the table top underneath. Remove and fix four strips of wood along the lines you have just drawn (to fit just outside the original area). Sand edges and cover with a tablecloth.

460 COTTON CLUB

Cotton furnishings are mostly machine washable (check the care label). Knitted cotton throws and cushion covers can be cleaned on a gentle cycle. Dry flat to retain their shape.

461 EXPERT ADVICE

Antique furniture repair is highly specialized so always consult a qualified expert especially if the piece is valuable. Over decades surface finishes develop their own patina – this is a sign of the age of a piece and should be preserved.

462 INSTANT AGEING

To give wooden furniture an attractive aged quality, mix varnish with soot and paint onto the surface.

463 FALSE ECONOMY

Buy the best sofa and/or armchairs you can afford. Budget buys can be uncomfortable and if it's not what you really want, you'll be keen to replace it as soon as you can. In small spaces, consider a good-quality sofa bed.

464 FAST & LOOSE

Loose covers may be laundered so they are a practical sofa solution. Protect vulnerable spots with arm and backguards. Throws are especially useful if you have children or pets.

465 GARDEN ROOM

Clean synthetic wicker garden furniture with a hose and plain water. Scrub stains with a stiff brush and a solution of washing-up liquid and water. Rinse and dry with a clean cloth.

466 IN THE CHAIR

Tighten up stretched and sagging cane by sponging carefully on the upper and lower sides with hot soapy water. Leave to dry away from heat and preferably in the open air, where they will shrink back to their original shape.

467 MAKE A SPLASH

Brighten up wooden furniture with a solution of water and vinegar. Soak a clean cloth in the solution and wash the piece all over, leave overnight to dry (with the window open, if you can). Next day apply quality furniture polish and buff away.

468 LOVING LEATHER

Minor spots may be cleaned with a little water (take care not to get the leather too damp) but for a more thorough clean, dust then apply saddle soap and dry thoroughly. Use leather conditioner on cracked furniture (test in an out-of-sight place first). Cracks may be prevented by rubbing leather every six months or so with a little castor oil.

469 MOVING HOUSE

When transporting furniture, remove drawers and lock doors so they don't open. Pad edges and cover. Wear clean white gloves (from chemists) to carry gilded items. Lift chairs by the seat, not the back or arms, and tables by the legs, not the top.

470 PREVENT POLISH BUILD-UP

Excess polish soon builds up and leaves a dull finish on wooden furniture. To remove it, mix together 2 tablespoons white vinegar and 2 tablespoons water. Apply to the surface and wipe off at once.

471 SAFE SHAMPOOING

Some sofas should be dry-cleaned by a professional – check the label. Otherwise use a commercial canned foaming shampoo. Follow the manufacturer's directions – usually the foam is left to stand until dry then vacuumed away.

472 NATURALLY NIFTY

Seek expert advice before cleaning antique wicker. Otherwise vacuum with the brush attachment. Wipe down with a damp cloth and warm, mild soapy water. Toothbrushes and stiff paintbrushes are useful for teasing dirt out of crevices. Hose down and dry in the sun, or with a hair dryer or fan. Avoid sitting in a wicker chair for two or three days after cleaning or you could cause sagging.

473 CURE SCRATCHES & DENTS

Treat scratched surfaces on wooden furniture by rubbing them with a halved Brazil nut. You can also get rid of small dents by placing a dampened cloth on top and running over them with a steam iron – don't try this on valuable pieces.

474 PERFECT PERSPEX

Glass and Perspex furniture creates a real sense of space in your home but needs to be cleaned regularly to look at its best. Using a spray bottle spritz a solution of one part white vinegar and four parts water onto a cloth. Rub into the glass taking care not to hold onto the article and create finger marks.

475 PROTECT PRECIOUS PIECES

Avoid placing wooden furniture near heat sources as this causes shrinkage and can loosen joints and veneers; also change the shape of the piece over time. Natural or artificial light alters finishes and can even break down the wood. Reduce light levels with curtains or blinds.

476 REVAMP WOOD

Greasy finger marks can be removed from wood with a damp cloth wrung in a mild solution of soap flakes. Dry thoroughly. Burnish out water and heat marks with cream metal polish. Working in small sections, rub briskly in the same direction as the grain and follow with a wax coating.

477 ROUGH PATCH

Mask light scratches on wooden furniture with shoe polish in a similar shade. Leave to absorb before buffing briskly.

478 LACQUERED LOOK

Wipe lacquered furniture with a damp (not wet) cloth. Dry with another clean cloth and buff to a shine with a soft cloth. An occasional polish adds shine to a dull surface.

479 ON YOUR MARKS

Banish rings left by cups and glasses on coffee tables and other surfaces by smearing them with petroleum jelly. Leave for 24 hours and then wipe off.

480 WASHING WOOL

Always wash wool according to the care label – unless mixed with synthetics it can often shrink in hot water. Washing can cause pilling so turn cushion covers inside out first. Blot stains quickly with kitchen towel – liquids penetrate the fibres slowly because of the natural oils contained in wool.

481 THE RIGHT CHOICE

Furniture oils and liquid wax are available in different wood colours so choose the correct one. Pale colours for wax and colourless oils are the safest options. Soften hardened wax by standing the tin in a jug of hot water for a few minutes but remember the tin will also conduct the heat, so hold with a cloth to remove.

482 WONDROUS WICKER

Keep furniture looking lovely by treating cracking and dryness with a solution of one part turpentine to two parts boiled linseed oil. Paint on as much as the wicker will absorb. Wipe away excess with a cloth. Dry for three or four days.

483 SPECIAL SHAMPOO

Make your own shampoo with ½ teaspoon washing-up liquid per litre (1¾ pints) of warm water. Squeeze the solution to create suds, scoop off the top and apply sparingly, one area at a time, with a sponge in the direction of the fabric grain. Avoid soaking. Make sure all suds are removed or dirt will stick to the residue.

484 COUCH CLEANER

A quick and easy way of freshening up
your sofa is to sprinkle a little baking soda
beneath the cushions. The baking soda
draws in the odour. Leave for at least
15 minutes then vacuum away.

485 SHABBY CHIC

Restore life and colour to leather with the occasional application of hide food or saddle soap. Buff well. Even if you love the look of worn leather, this treatment slows down the process of deterioration.

486 SIMPLE MOISTURIZER

Serious marks on leather may be treated with moisturizing soap. Simply wipe a cloth over the bar of soap then rub clean and buff.

487 SUMMER TIME

If you have upholstered your sofa(s) in dark colours, have an extra set of loose covers made up in heavy white cotton or a pastel shade for the summer. Swap cushions and curtains seasonally, too.

488 LOOKING AFTER ANTIQUES

All furniture, but especially antique pieces, should be kept away from direct sources of heat and light. Always check with the seller how to clean it, or consult an expert for further advice. Damaged pieces should be professionally restored.

489 SOFA, SO GOOD

Prevent dust and dust mites by regularly vacuuming your sofa. Moistened or ground-in dust can stain upholstery. Use the upholstery attachment and a gentle brush plus the crevice tool attachment for nooks and crannies. Or brush dust away with a soft-bristled brush – especially suitable for feather-filled sofas that will not respond well to vacuuming.

490 SOMETHING IN DISGUISE

Hide scratches on wood with crayons and try iodine on darker woods such as cherry and mahogany. Place on a clean cloth or cotton wool and apply sparingly.

491 WATERCOLOUR WONDER

If the scratch has not gone through to the wood, surface finishes of varnish, shellac or wax can be repaired. Be sure the area is dust-free and with a sable brush and basic watercolour set, match colours first by painting on an area that can't be seen. Keep a clean cloth ready to dry stray spots. When dry, polish with beeswax and a lint-free cloth.

482 YOU GLOW, GIRL!

Buffing achieves a reflective glow on surfaces and furniture. Use good lint-free cloths made of linen or cotton that are soft and woven. Remove surface dirt with a damp cloth. Dry and rub briskly. Fold or gather cloth to make a thick wad that gives more power to your elbow. Always go with the grain when buffing wood.

483 TOP TABLES

Avoid scratches on glass tables by using mats and tablecloths. Remove smears and grease with hot soapy water and polish dry. A little methylated spirit on a clean cloth removes grease and adds sparkle. Non-gel toothpaste may remove some scratches. File chips with fine emery paper, but be careful of the surrounding surface and your fingers!

484 STOP DRAWERS STICKING

Rub a wax candle across the runners of a drawer that keeps sticking. It's amazing the difference this will make.

485 UPHOLSTERY UPKEEP

Shampooing once a year protects upholstery fabric, but make sure you check the labels first. To avoid shrinkage, wash covers in a mild solution of shampoo and water and, after ironing gently on the wrong side to prevent shine, replace them while they are still just damp. To remove dirt from delicate upholstery use a soft brush dipped in shampoo foam (follow the manufacturer's instructions). Rinse with a cloth dampened in clean water. Dry, then vacuum.

486 STAIN SOLUTIONS

Marks on light-coloured wood can usually be removed by dipping a cloth in wood cleaner and working with the grain. Buff with a cloth and apply furniture polish. Alternatively, try a mix of 50:50 baking soda and white toothpaste or leave mayonnaise on the stain for an hour. On light carpets and upholstery, wet a cloth in 50:50 water/white vinegar and blot the surface gently.

lighting

497 GIN PALACE

Intricate glass chandeliers can be cleaned with neat gin and a soft cloth to get them gleaming again.

498 LIGHT FANTASTIC

Pale ceilings, walls and furnishings enhance reflected light and make the most of it. To spread light over larger areas of a room, use diffusers.

499 LIGHTEN UP

Serious dirt on shades can be cleaned with a dry-cleaning sponge (from DIY stores). Use as an eraser and instead of water on paper shades and those with glue.

500 SQUEAKY CLEAN

Dust glass or plastic lampshades regularly – if necessary wash them with a clean cloth and detergent solution. Brush parchment and paper with a feather duster. Vacuum raffia, straw and fabric lights with low power suction.

501 THE RIGHT LOCATION

Place lights where you need them and use spot and desk lights for close work such as sewing and reading. Avoid glare by covering them with a shade.

502 GLASS GLOBES

Clean glass bases and globes with washing-up liquid and water, or hot water and a dash of ammonia. Provided parts don't have electrical connectors, it's safe to immerse them. Otherwise, wipe with a cloth dipped in the soapy solution and wrung dry.

503 GIVE FABRIC THE BRUSH-OFF

After dusting with a soft-bristled paintbrush, use a dry-cleaning sponge (available from DIY stores) in the same way as an eraser to remove surface dirt on fabric lampshades.

504 ALTERED IMAGE

Add atmosphere with table, wall and floor lamps or concealed lighting. For softer, more diffused lighting, use lower wattage and pearl bulbs.

505 CLEANING CRYSTAL CHANDELIERS

Switch off first and lightly dampen a chamois with water. Wipe down the crystal while attached to the frame and the chandelier itself with a dry cloth. If the crystal is really dirty, remove and soak in a combination of warm water, 1 ½ tablespoons of white vinegar and 1 drop of washing-up liquid. Rinse under running water and buff with a soft cloth.

506 PERFECT PLEATS

Remove dust trapped in a pleated lampshade with a small, clean medium-bristled paintbrush. This works well with trinkets and bric-a-brac, too.

office & study

507 BE YOUR OWN BANKER

Have bank statements sent to your home once a month and spend an hour or so checking your account against cheques going out and money withdrawn. Keep a list of outgoings and when you get paid, deduct this from your salary so you always know exactly how much money you have to spare.

508 KEYBOARD CARE

Occasionally turn your keyboard upside down to dislodge crumbs and dust. If particles settle, faults may occur. Turn the keyboard the right way round again and dust keys with a small, soft paintbrush – if very dusty, use canned air for this.

509 CONCERTINA STYLE

Keep a file full of appliance guarantees, bank statements, paid bills (date these), mortgage agreements, and so forth so you can lay your hands on important paperwork in minutes.

510 MANAGE THE HOUSEKEEPING

Throughout the month as you receive bills place them in a clear plastic folder and when you get paid, sit down and pay them all at once, then file them. Alternatively set up direct debits so you can pay little and often and avoid huge heating or phone bills.

511 KEEP A CLIPPINGS FILE

Magazines can take up valuable space so start a clippings file for useful articles and also information downloaded from the Internet that you might want to refer back to at some stage. Use dividers to arrange everything so it's easily accessible.

512 DESK-TOP POLISHING

Use non-abrasive all-purpose cleaner to remove ink and felt-tip pen marks from varnished or laminated wood. Remove rubber-based white glue with soap suds – don't scour, just wait for it to be dissolved. Scrape away blobs of solvent based glue with a small paint scraper and dissolve the residue with nail polish remover.

513 MOUSE MAINTENANCE

To keep your mouse manoeuvring well, every so often remove the track ball cover. Take out the track ball and clean inside with a cotton wool swab dampened with alcohol. Replace and cover.

514 PERSONAL TOUCH

Surround yourself with attractive desk kits and stationery and you'll find working at home is far more fun. Alter the colour of your computer screen or choose a relaxing image such as a photo of the sea or lush leaves for a screensaver.

515 POSITION WELL

Place your computer where air can circulate around it and away from direct sunlight and heat. Dust regularly around buttons and keys with a soft cloth and synthetic paintbrush.

516 OZONE SAFE

Work in a well-ventilated room and turn off computers and printers when not in use as they produce ozone. Ensure adequate lighting by placing your desk close to a window with the computer screen at right angles to it.

517 POISED FOR A TAKEOVER

Make sure your desk chair is the correct height and provides adequate support for your lower back. Adjustable chairs on castors allow flexibility of movement and positioning. If you're concerned about hunched shoulders, sit on a Swiss ball to keep you poised and maximize core body strength.

518 SCHEDULE IT IN

Keep a calendar in order to organize and keep track of the busy life of your family – some paper calendars are now divided into columns for each family member. Alternatively, use a software calendar program that you can transfer to cell phones, PDAs and other computers via an iPod or USB thumb drive.

519 YOU HAVE MAIL

Manage your in-box. Transfer addresses, phone numbers and important dates to your diary as well as your online address book so you can still contact everyone if your computer crashes. Delete anything you don't need as you go along.

sweet scents

520 FAST FREEZE

Candles last longer if you place them in the freezer for at least three hours prior to burning.

521 AN APPLE A DAY

It's amazing, but true, sliced apples will remove the smell of cigarette smoke in an enclosed area. Try placing a bowl of apple slices on a table or mantelpiece.

INSTANT AROMA

Toss a sheet of fabric softener
in the wastebasket for a
fresh clean fragrance. Or
dab a little perfume on a
light bulb – it floods the
room with scent when the
light is turned on.

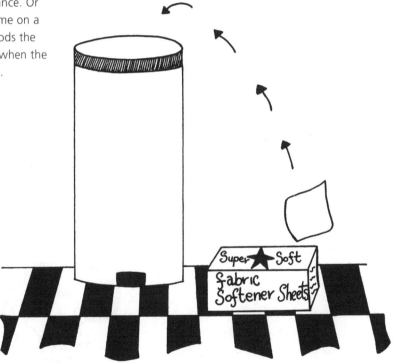

523 FRESH AS A DAISY

Vanilla essence absorbs strong smells such as new paint and even last night's curry. Simply add 2–3 teaspoons to a saucer to release the fragrance. Baking soda sprinkled in an ashtray also absorbs cigarette-ash fragrance in no time.

524 SCENT SURROUND

Warm spicy air spray fragrances work well in winter living rooms and hallways while citrus fresh notes are perfect for spring and summer. Combine with scented candles for a layered effect.

525 WARM WELCOME

Create an instant ambience by placing potpourri in glass or leather bowls. Remember to turn it regularly though or it will attract dust. Refresh with essential oils.

526 QUICK SOAK

Cheap candles have a tendency to drip so try placing them in water just deep enough to cover them. Add 2 teaspoons of salt and soak for an hour or so.

527 SIMPLY STYLISH

Dot a few candles around the living room and light them just before guests arrive. Spray your favourite scent around the room, plump up the pillows and straighten the rug. Fresh flowers make any room special so treat yourself (and your home) to a regular supply.

528 FILL YOUR HOME WITH FLOWERS

Alternatively, buy scented candles and enjoy delicious wafts of fragrance without enormous florist's bills. Calming, alluring or invigorating – choose a scent to create atmosphere in every room of your home.

detergents

529 DETERGENT CHOICES

Mostly you'll need just one detergent for the machine and a gentler one for hand-washing. Powder is economical but messy, liquid dissolves easily and tablets save space but are costly. Follow the manufacturer's recommendations for best results.

530 DON'T GET IN A LATHER

Use a gentle detergent that's suitable for hand-washing cashmere, wool and silk in warm water and make sure the detergent has dissolved first. Wash lights and darks in separate water and avoid wringing delicates and woollens.

531 GO GREEN

Try a laundry ball instead of power or liquid detergent. It produces ionized oxygen that activates water molecules allowing them to penetrate deeply into fibres to shift dirt. Hypoallergenic, they are suitable for sensitive skin and save water. What's more, they can be used up to 750 times.

drying clothes

532 CASHMERE CARE

If hand-washing, reshape while damp and dry flat on a plain towel. Store cashmere in summer months wrapped in acid-free tissue in boxes to prevent moths.

533 HANG IT ALL

Before you begin to hang clothes check your line and pegs are clean and free from rust, which could cause stains. Hang whites in direct sunlight to brighten them but leave colours in shaded areas.

534 DON'T GET IN A SPIN

Never spin-dry Lycra or stretch fabrics or you could end up with garments that are at best completely out of shape and at worst, double the size!

535 DON'T OVERHEAT

Avoid drying laundry beside a radiator – the heat can damage some fabrics. Don't set the timer on a tumble dryer to run more than 30 minutes before checking it either.

536 SARTORIAL STYLE

Try a trick favoured by stylists: wash and then hang a silk dress or camisole on a padded hanger to dry. The air will circulate around it on all sides so it dries quickly.

537 INDOOR DRYING

If you live in a city you may not have access to outdoor space in which to hang your clothes to dry, so give washed clothes a vigorous shake and reshape before hanging on a clothes rack. Dry delicates and knitwear flat on colourfast towels out of direct sunlight.

538 ON THE LINE

If you have to dry clothes indoors use a wall-mounted airer. Simply mount it on a wall over the bath to catch drips, pull out the lines and hook to a bracket on the opposite wall. The airer automatically rewinds after use. Remember to spin clothes well or you will put strain on the fixings.

539 ZAP MILDEW

Dry clothes soon after washing. Place chemical absorbers (available from chemists) in damp cupboards – or make your own by tying several sticks of chalk together and hanging in the cupboard to absorb moisture.

540 BEAUTIFUL BLANKETS

You can tumble-dry wool blankets but only on the 'no heat' or 'air' setting. If you have access to outdoor space, save energy by hanging them over two tightly strung clotheslines.

ironing

541 DELICATELY DOES IT

Iron silk, delicates and surface decoration with a protective cloth on top. If you iron inside out, this protects the fabric from the heat and also prevents it becoming shiny. Press lightly.

542 DELIGHTFULLY DECADENT

Add a touch of luxury to your linens by using delicate scented sprays when ironing. Many designer perfume houses are now creating their own lines in a range of fragrances from lime and orange blossom to lavender. As you iron, the room will fill with fragrance.

543 A LITTLE PRESSING

Tailored items require pressing rather than ironing. This is best done professionally, but you can touch up a garment such as a suit at home. Take a hot iron and a damp calico or linen cloth. Place the cloth on the garment and press heavily to remove creases. Continue pressing until the cloth is dry – be careful not to touch the garment directly with the iron or shiny patches may appear.

544 GET SHIRTY

To iron a perfect shirt, first shake and place on a hanger to shape as it dries. Spray liberally with ironing water. Begin by ironing the collar on the wrong side, outer corner in. Repeat on the right side. Now iron the yoke, wrong side first and then right side. Follow with the cuffs (wrong and right side), back, sleeves and two fronts working around buttons. Air on a hanger before returning to the closet.

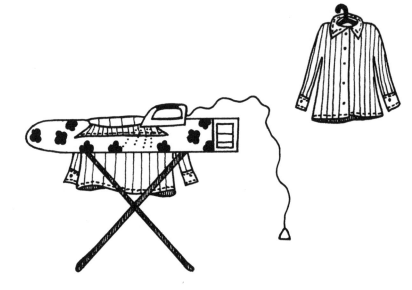

545 AVOID EXCESSIVE IRONING

Smooth and fold clothes carefully when you take them off the line or out of the drier to keep ironing to a minimum. If this is your least favourite chore, choose non-iron bed linen, too.

546 BUTTON MANOEUVRES

Work carefully around buttons with the tip of the iron. If you iron the buttons you may melt them and you will also mark the fabric.

547 CAN'T STAND CREASES?

Generously splash dry, creased linen or cotton with water and roll up for an hour or two before ironing. The moisture will spread through the fibres and help ease ironing. For best results, iron garments while still damp.

548 COVER CARE

Extend the life of your new ironing board cover by spraying it liberally with spray starch. Finish off by ironing over the surface on high heat.

549 CURE SCORCH MARKS

If you iron on too high a setting, you run the risk of scorch marks. If the affected item is 100 per cent cotton, soak the scorched area in pure, freshly squeezed lemon juice. Rinse out thoroughly in warm water and leave outside to bleach naturally in the sunlight.

550 EASIER IRONING

Minimize creases by gently pulling garments into shape and neatly folding them in a basket before ironing. Double-fold sheets and large cloths so it's simpler to work the iron around them.

551 THE HEAT IS ON

Leave the iron to warm up on the cool setting for at least five minutes after you've switched it on. This gives the thermostat time to settle and the sole plate will heat up evenly. Begin with items such as fine silks that require the coolest setting and increase the heat gradually until you get to more robust cottons and linens.

552 KITTING OUT KIDS

Spend less time at the ironing board by buying kids' clothes in easy-care, drip-dry fabrics that don't require ironing. Fold their T-shirts and sweatshirts while slightly damp, smooth flat then leave to dry in the airing cupboard and you won't need to iron them at all.

553 PRACTICE MAKES PERFECT

Learn how to iron well in order to cut down on ironing time. Press clothes according to how they are constructed. For example, work carefully in the direction of darts or gathers and spend time reintroducing pleats.

554 PERFECT PANTS

For boardroom trousers, first iron the pockets then fit the top part of the trousers over the end of the ironing board and iron. Fold the them lengthways so the seams are to the middle and creases at the outside edges. Iron inside then outside the leg. Turn the trousers over and iron the other leg in the same way.

555 DETAILS COUNT

Before ironing napkins, handkerchiefs, scarves and other small items, pull them into shape first. Tack pleats in skirts or trousers in place prior to ironing and always press embossed cottons on the wrong side.

556 PREVENT LIMESCALE

Take care of your steam iron by always adding distilled water and not using water straight from the tap (faucet). This stops limescale building up. Or use filtered water from a filter jug.

557 SHABBY CHIC

No time to iron the sheets? When bed linens are dry, pull them into shape, fold up carefully and then place at the bottom of the linen pile to flatten them.

558 TABLE LINEN TREATMENTS

If you're ironing a round tablecloth, start in the centre and work outwards. Always iron napkins flat – never iron in creases. Damask is designed to be shiny so to maintain this, iron on the wrong side first and then on the right side.

559 START STARCHING

Most fabrics wear better when starched and starch adds a soft gloss to cotton and helps keep out dirt especially around collars. Too much starch, however, can cause fabrics to crack and become dry so follow the manufacturer's advice. Spray starch is the most timesaving type.

560 VELVET TOUCH

Never iron velvet or you will damage the surface. Instead hold it over a steaming kettle and stretch it wherever crease marks have appeared.

561 GOOD FOIL

Place a sheet of foil beneath your ironing board cover. This will reflect the heat and also saves energy.

562 CUT DOWN ON CREASES

To iron a table cloth effectively, place a table next to your ironing board. Allow cloth to drape over the table but don't let it drag on the floor as you iron.

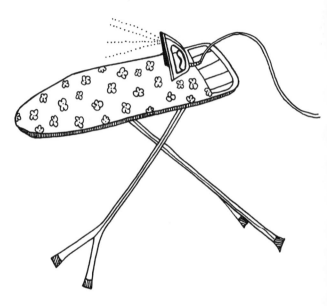

563 FUN WHILE YOU WORK

Choose a good-quality iron and board plus a pretty cover and have a radio on in the background to make ironing more fun.

564 SOLE SURVIVAL

If you've used the iron on too-high heat and something's got stuck, unplug it and cool. On aluminium and chrome sole plates apply a paste of bicarbonate of soda and water to the consistency of toothpaste with a soft cloth. Wipe away with a damp cloth. Treat Teflon or metallic-coated plates by rubbing a nylon scourer over the surface when cool.

565 UNCLOG YOUR STEAM IRON

Pour equal amounts of vinegar and water into the water holder of the iron. Turn the dial to steam and leave upright for five minutes. Unplug and let the iron cool down. Any loose particles should fall out when you empty the water.

fabric care

566 ACETATE

Satin, taffeta, brocades and often linings are made from acetate. Wash in warm water on the delicate programme. Do not spin and iron on a cool setting.

567 ACRYLIC

Used often as an alternative to wool. Wash in warm water on a synthetics programme on a short spin. Reduce static by adding fabric conditioner to the last rinse. Do not wring; use a cool iron without the steam setting. Shape when wet and dry flat.

568 ANGORA

Hand-wash and treat as for wool. To prevent moulting, store wrapped in a plastic bag in the fridge or freezer before wearing if you have the space.

569 ANTIQUE LACE

Wash in a mild detergent and dry flat. Seek professional advice before cleaning precious pieces.

570 BROCADE

Heavy stiff fabric often used for upholstery and soft furnishings. Dry-clean only and use a cool iron on the reverse side.

571 BRODERIE ANGLAISE

Treat according to fabric type and the care label. Wash delicate pieces by hand or place in a muslin bag before machine washing.

572 CALICO

Wash as cotton (see below). Whiten unbleached calico by adding bleach to the first wash. Be sure to rinse thoroughly.

573 CASHMERE

Hand-wash or dry-clean – the choice is yours. Some brave creatures will even wash on a wool setting in the machine. Whatever you do, stick to the same cleaning method. If hand-washing, use a mild detergent in cool water and never wring. Avoid softener as this causes felting.

574 CHENILLE

Wash according to fabric type or dry-clean.

575 CHIFFON

Wash according to fibre type or dry-clean. Do not spin or wring. While damp, iron gently with a cool iron.

576 CHINTZ

Best dry-cleaned only, however the glaze will be removed with continuous cleaning.

577 CORDUROY

Use a synthetics programme with a minimal spin to protect the pile. Trousers should be washed inside out. Iron on the reverse while damp on a steam setting. Brush up the pile gently.

578 COTTON

Different qualities and weights of cotton are available. Machine washable but may fade or shrink if washed above 40 °C (104 °F). Iron on a steam setting while damp. Avoid greying by always using the recommended dosage instructions for the programme and products. Do not overload the machine.

578 CREPE DE CHINE

Hand-wash according to fibre type. Rinse in cold water and roll the fabric in a towel to remove any excess water. Iron gently on the cool setting.

580 DAMASK

Often used for table linen. Wash according to fibre type. Heavier items should be dry-cleaned.

581 DENIM

If not preshrunk, use a cool wash. Always turn inside out and wash separately to avoid colour running. Iron on the maximum or steam setting while damp.

582 ELASTANES/LYCRA

Machine wash on a low temperature using a delicate programme. Alternatively hand-wash in warm water, rinse and run through a short spin or roll in a towel. Do not tumble dry.

583 FELT/FLANNEL/GABERDINE

Dry-clean only.

584 GEORGETTE

Dry-clean natural fabrics such as cotton, silk and wool – man-made items may be washed according to fibre type.

585 GINGHAM

Check for colourfastness and then wash according to fibre type. While damp press with a steam iron.

586 GROSGRAIN

This fine, ribbed fabric should be washed according to fabric type or alternatively dry-cleaned.

587 JERSEY

Wash according to fibre type or dry clean. Use a short spin and dry flat, shaping while wet. Reverse steam iron.

588 LACE

Place in a muslin bag or pillowcase then machine-wash according to fibre type with a gentle non-biological powder. Iron on the wrong side while damp, pulling to shape.

589 LINEN

Dry-clean garments with anti-crease finishes. Others can be placed in a hot wash and spin dry. Hang to dry then iron on the reverse while it is still damp with a hot steam iron. To add extra body to the garment, starch occasionally.

590 MOHAIR

This light woven fabric is often mixed with other fibres. Hand-wash and treat as wool.

591 MOIRE

Dry clean only and do not steam iron.

592 MUSLIN

Hand wash open-weave sheer cotton in warm water. Do not spin the item, rather dry it flat. While it is damp, iron on a medium setting.

593 NUBUCK

Specialist nubuck and calf-leather cleaners require no brushing – suede shampoos and brushes will damage the pile.

594 NYLON/POLYAMIDE

For flame-resistant fabric, wash in hand-hot water, or a delicate programme, with a fabric conditioner to reduce static. Cold rinse, short spin and drip-dry. Use a cool iron if necessary. Colours should be washed separately as dye can be absorbed easily by this fabric. Avoid bleaching, direct heat or sunlight.

595 PERCALE

Fine cotton or polyester cotton is often used for bedding. Wash the item according to fibre type.

596 POLYESTER/TREVIRA

Wash on a synthetics programme with a short spin and fabric conditioner in the final rinse. Tumble-dry, if necessary. Hand-wash pleated items and drip-dry, preferably outside.

597 POPLIN

Wash or clean this closely woven cotton (silk, wool or viscose) according to the fibre type.

598 PVC

Gently sponge away marks with diluted washing-up liquid. If necessary, hand-wash in warm water and, if possible, drip dry outdoors on a washing line. PVC melts under direct heat so make sure you never iron or dry-clean it.

599 SATIN

Wash according to fibre type (silk, cotton, polyester, acetate or polyamide). Reverse iron while damp until dry. Heavier items should be dry-cleaned.

600 SHANTUNG

Washed this slubbed silk according to fibre type (silk, acetate or polyamide).

601 SHEEPSKIN

Apply a protective spray to a sheepskin item to avoid marking and staining, and dry-clean the garment regularly. Small areas may be cleaned with suede cleaner, but make sure you test it first. Dry shampoo marks on the wool side. Rugs are best cleaned professionally.

602 SILK

Wash in mild liquid detergent those items that are clearly marked hand-wash, but never hand-wash anything labelled dry-clean only. Biological detergents, heat and washing soda damage the fibres of the fabric, as does wringing or rubbing. Add fabric conditioner to the final rinse and roll in a clean dry towel to remove surplus water.

603 SUEDE

Apply a waterproof spray (make sure you test it on a small, hidden patch first) to new or newly cleaned suede. This will prevent the colour from rubbing off. Dirty or rain-spotted suede may be wiped with a clean damp cloth then dried naturally. Brush often with a suede block or wire brush. Serious stains, marks or discoloration should be professionally treated.

604 TAFFETA/PRINTED SILK

Dry-clean only and iron carefully on the reverse side.

605 TOWELLING

Machine wash dark colours separately on a cotton programme. Give nappies a hot wash with fabric conditioner on the final rinse. Soak stiff, rough towels overnight in water-softener, then machine wash with maximum detergent. Tumble-dry and use fabric softener every third wash to keep towelling soft and fluffy.

606 TULLE

Dry-clean silk tulle otherwise hand-wash according to fibre type (cotton, polyamide or viscose). Limp cotton tulle may be starched to give it some body. Stiffen nylon or viscose tulle with gum arabic solution (from health stores).

607 TWEED/VELOUR

Dry-clean both of these fabrics only. Iron velour on the reverse side with a cool iron.

608 VELVET

Treat according to fibre (silk, cotton or manmade) or dry-clean. Shake occasionally while drying. Restore pile with a soft cloth or velvet brush. Between wear, creases can be steamed out. Iron with the pile face down on a soft cloth.

609 VISCOSE

Also known as rayon, wash with care at low temperatures. Discourage creasing with a short spin – do not wring. While damp iron on a steam setting.

610 VIYELLA

Wash by hand in hand-hot water. Squeeze gently or roll in a towel to remove water; do not spin. While damp, iron on the reverse.

611 WOOL

Hand-wash carefully with gentle detergent and warm water. Do not twist, wring or rub. Dry flat between two towels and correct the shape while damp. Never tumble-dry. If the care label states that the garment is machine washable, use the woollens programme.

machine care

612 QUICK RINSE

To clean out the walls of your washing machine, use the hottest water and ammonia. Put through a couple of cycles without soap or clothes. Periodically pour a cup of vinegar or 200 ml (7 fl oz) bleach into the machine and let it run through on the hottest cycle to dissolve soap residue.

613 MACHINE MAINTENANCE

Stand your washing machine and tumble dryer on a sturdy, even surface to avoid damage during the wash cycle. Regularly clean the soap drawer to prevent powder build-up. Each month empty the filter of the washing machine and to avoid limescale, add a handful of soda crystals to each wash. Lastly, have both machines serviced regularly.

614 CLEAN MACHINE

Every so often wipe down the outside of your washing machine and tumble dryer with warm soapy water to get rid of dirt, accumulated dust and spilled products.

615 EFFICIENT FILTERING

Keep the filter of your tumble dryer clean but also check that the duct allowing the air outside isn't blocked. Once a year detach it from the back of your dryer and clean it. Be sure the vent cover is in place or buy a replacement from a DIY store. After every use empty the water container of condenser dryer.

616 LOOK AFTER THE PENNIES

It makes sense to be economical when washing and only wash when you have a full load. Today's programmes are just as effective at low temperatures. You can also save money by drying clothes outdoors on a line instead of using your tumble dryer.

617 CHECK THE MANUAL

Most tumble dryers have alerts to remind you to clean filters collecting lint before or after every load of clothes. Follow the manufacturer's instructions for this. Once removed, hold the filter over the bin while scraping lint away with your hand. Wash stubborn lint away with warm soapy water and then rinse.

618 KIDS' SCRIBBLES

If the kids have been playing and you later discover crayon marks inside the dryer, don't despair. Soften marks by running the machine on empty for five minutes. Then wipe with a cloth and warm soapy water.

619 REDUCE CALCIUM DEPOSITS

Add 1–2 tablespoons washing soda to the detergent drawer of your washing machine. You'll also reduce the amount of commercial powder needed by 30 percent.

mending & repairing

620 SEIZE THE DAY

Carry out repairs as soon as possible or the situation may worsen – loose seams, small tears and torn fabric could be damaged irreparably, especially if you put them through a wash prior to sewing.

621 A STITCH IN TIME

Spray hair lacquer onto the end of a strand of cotton to stiffen it so threading needles becomes easier.

622 DEALING WITH DYE

For a white wash, check the item is not nylon and can be bleached to remove the dye transfer. Soak in a weak solution of bleach (25 ml (1 fl oz) to 5 litres (8 pints) water) for 15 minutes. Rinse by hand or use the rinse programme on your machine. Repeat as necessary. On coloured fabrics, try a proprietary colour run remover but test on a hidden area first.

623 BUTTON UP

If a button has fallen off recently you can see where to re-attach it. Otherwise mark the spot with a pin or chalk. Sew with double thread for stronger stitches. Knot the end, trim away excess and sew through from the wrong side before you add your button. Loop in and out of the starting point until the button is secure. Sew through on the wrong side to secure and trim away excess thread.

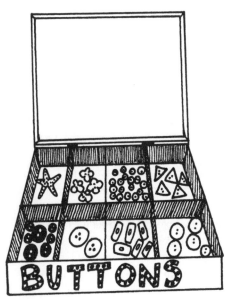

625 HAVE A BUTTON BOX

Keep spare buttons – especially ones from favourite garments – in a button box so you don't lose them. Store spare beads and decorations, too.

626 HOW TO HEM

First pin the garment to the length you want it to be – it's best to ask a friend to do this while you are wearing it plus the accompanying shoes. Fold the fabric once and then again. Sew with tacking thread in a contrasting colour. Now thread your needle with matching thread and stitch through the folded side in a zig-zag. Continue all the way round, secure and trim. Gently press for a sharper line.

624 SEAMLESS FINISH

Because machine-made stitches are stronger, it's best to have seams professionally repaired. In an emergency you can secure a hem with clear plastic tape (keep some in your bag), which will last a few hours.

627 PREVENT PILLING

As pilling is caused by friction, it's hard to stop this happening especially around the sleeves of sweaters. Remove fibre balls easily and prolong the life of garments with a hand-held defuzzer or electric machine (from department stores).

soft & fragrant

628 KEEP A KIT

Have a pretty tin or basket dedicated to all your sewing needs. Include needles, a thimble, pins, a sharp pair of scissors and tape measure, thread in neutral shades and any other colours you might use. Safety pins, Velcro and tailor's chalk could all be useful, too.

629 NATURAL FABRIC CONDITIONER

Mix together 1 cup each washing soda, white vinegar and water. Sir in a few drops of essential oil such as lavender, lemon or geranium. Store in a screw-top bottle and use as commercial conditioner.

630 SOFT TOUCH

Place fabric softener sheets in drawers and your clothes will smell freshly washed for weeks to come. You can also do this with towels and linen.

631 SPEND LESS

Fabric conditioners in a range of new fragrances are now available in concentrated form which means a smaller quantity is necessary. What's more, it's less harmful to the environment.

632 STEAM AWAY SMOKE

To remove the smoke smell from clothes after a night out, add a cup of vinegar to a bathtub of hot water. Hang the clothes above the steam.

633 SWEET SMELLS

To deliciously scent clothes, use a fabric conditioner in your wash and fill your steam iron with scented linen water – this also makes ironing easier.

special care

634 ACT FAST

Take stained clothes that are dry-clean only to the cleaners as soon as possible or you run the risk of the stain being impossible to remove later on. Make sure you always point out the location of the stains to the dry cleaners.

635 DRY CLEANING LABELS

Study the care label on your garments if you leave them with a dry cleaner. Unless the label clearly states 'dry-clean only', the company may refuse to take responsibility for any damage. Choose a reputable company – a cheap one could ultimately prove costly.

636 AFTER-WEAR

Brush clothes after use and spot-clean to avoid unnecessary trips to the dry cleaners. If clothes come back smelling of solvent, remove the packaging to allow them to breathe and air-clean before returning to your closet.

637 MOTHBALL MIRACLE

It's true – odourless mothballs have arrived! Available in drycleaners, they can be stored in boxes or hung round hangers. At last your clothes can be protected without becoming fusty.

638 ON THE BUTTON

If your clothes have metallic or particularly special buttons or fastenings, cover them in aluminium foil to protect them before your clothes are dry-cleaned.

639 NEW LEASE OF LIFE

To give velvet and satin garments a lift, hang and steam them. Brush velvet with still more velvet to refresh the pile.

640 ZIPPERED ITEMS

Here's how to clean zips on large items including tents, wetsuits and suitcases. First dip a toothbrush in a solution of a little washing-up liquid and warm water and brush away any dirt. Rinse in plain water and leave open until the zip has dried.

641 KEEP SLIDERS SMOOTH

Rub a wax candle along the zip teeth and work in the wax by moving the slider up and down several times. White candles are best: you don't want to smear dye around. Wipe away excess wax.

642 ZIP CARE

Wash zips in washable items with water and detergent suitable for the fabric. Zip up before placing garments in the washing machine to protect both the machine and the zip. Keep the zip closed while ironing to protect it and work round it carefully – excessive heat can damage and even destroy plastic and polyester.

643 LOVING CARE

Always have wedding dresses (also veils and christening gowns) professionally dry-cleaned prior to storage even if they do not seem visibly dirty. Colourless stains such as perfume can develop and discolour fabrics as they react with the air and these stains can never be removed.

644 NEXT GENERATION

Consider professional vacuum packing to preserve your wedding gown or any other precious item of clothing for at least 25 years. If you remove the dress before then the preserving properties will be lost, however.

645 MEMORY BOX

Store your bridal gown in a special acid-reduced box interleaved with acid-free tissue. Do not use ordinary cardboard, plastic bags or PVC zipped covers – chemicals from these packaging materials can leak through the tissue. Put the box in a cool cupboard away from damp, direct or indirect heat and sunlight. Every 18 months to two years refold your dress along slightly different lines to help prevent permanent creases.

super stain removers

646 BABY OIL/HAIR OIL

Rub mild liquid detergent into the stain. Leave for 15 minutes and then wash as normal.

647 BALLPOINT PEN MARKS

Apply methylated spirits to the stain and rinse thoroughly. Or try rubbing the affected area with a cotton bud soaked in eau de cologne. Wash as normal.

648 BEER

Apply vinegar and then rinse. Treat with liquid detergent and rinse. Lukewarm water and salt is also known to work. If the stain remains, treat with hydrogen peroxide (test the fabric first) and rinse. Washable fabrics may be washed at high temperature. Bleach by drying in the sun.

649 BERRIES

Berry stains are considered dye stains and consequently tough to remove. Pre-treat washable garments with commercial stain remover then soak in a diluted solution of oxygen bleach (25 ml (1 fl oz) to 2 litres (3½ pints) of water. Machine wash on the maximum temperature. A solvent of methylated spirits may work on dry-clean only clothes. Dab at the stain with a cotton bud and a dash of solution.

650 BLOOD STAINS

Pour a little hydrogen peroxide on a cloth and then proceed to wipe away the stain – works every time! This also removes mustard and grass stains. Or soak overnight in a solution of half a cup of salt mixed in a medium-sized bucket with water. Wash as normal.

651 CANDLE WAX

Freeze the garment for an hour or so (this allows the pieces to be cracked off). Sandwich residue between clean brown paper and iron with a warm iron. Dry-cleaning solvent will get rid of remnants. Treat colour from the wax with white spirit and then rinse.

652 CHOCOLATE

Remove the excess by scraping at it with a blunt knife. Rinse in cold water and treat with liquid detergent. Rinse. If the stain still lingers, apply a dry-cleaning solvent.

653 COFFEE/TEA

Run under the cold tap (faucet). If the stain persists soak in hand-hot liquid detergent; rinse thoroughly. Any remnants may be treated when dry with a solution of half hydrogen peroxide, half water.

654 COOKING OIL

On dry-clean only clothes blot the grease with paper towels dampened with acetone-based nail polish remover (do not use on acetate or it will dissolve). Treat washable items with commercial pre-wash stain remover and biological liquid detergent. After pre-treatment, wash immediately in hot water safe enough for the fabric and colours.

655 CREAM

Rinse the stain in cold water then treat with liquid detergent. Rinse thoroughly.

656 CURRY

Soak in white spirit or diluted household ammonia. If the stain remains, check the care label and if the fabric is strong enough, bleach.

657 DEODORANT

Anti-perspirant and deodorant stains on silk can damage it so dry-clean or wash garments as soon as possible. Try this trick: dissolve 2 aspirins in 100 ml (3½ fl oz) warm water and apply to the stain (test on a hidden spot first to see if the fabric holds). Dry for four hours, brush off and launder. Or soak in water and a paste of table salt and vinegar.

658 FELT-TIP PEN

Lubricate the stain with hard soap and wash as normal. Apply methylated spirits to stubborn stains and wash again to remove any final traces.

659 FRESH FRUIT

While new, cover the stain in salt and wash without soap (the alkali in the soap will fix the stain).

660 GLUE

First check the label or packaging for advice from the manufacturers. Generally, PVA glue may be removed with methylated spirit while contact adhesives can be treated with non-oily nail polish remover.

GRASS

Daub delicates with methylated spirits on a clean cloth. If the fabric can be laundered, soak in cold water, cover with a little cream of tartar and leave in the sun.

662 GREASY MARKS

Blot stains on satin with a clean white rag then cover with flour or unscented talcum powder and leave for an hour. The powder will absorb most of the stain. Gently brush with a soft-bristled brush and launder according to the care label.

663 GREASE ON SUEDE

Get rid of greasy marks on suede by dipping a toothbrush in vinegar and gently brushing it over the grease spot.

664 HAIR LACQUER/NAIL VARNISH

Apply amyl acetate (non-oily nail polish remover) and wash as normal.

ICE CREAM

Remove the excess with a spoon and soak in a solution of warm detergent. If the stain lingers, treat with dry-cleaning solvent.

INK

To remove ink stains from fabric or leather, spray hair spray lavishly on the area and wipe with a clean rag. Wash fabric afterwards according to the care label. Stains on shirts can be removed by soaking in milk overnight then washing the next day.

667 JAMS & PRESERVES

Flush with cold water and treat with liquid detergent. Rinse. For persistent stains, treat with white spirit and rinse again. If necessary, soak in liquid detergent solution, rinse and wash as normal.

668 KIDS' URINE

Accidents will happen and sometimes kids wet the bed. To eliminate the smell, just add a can of cheap cola to your wash.

669 LIPSTICK

Toothpaste will remove lipstick stains. Rub into the stain as a pre-treatment and wash as normal. Or try dry-cleaning solvent on washable fabrics, then rub with liquid detergent and scrub in hot water. Wash as the care label with a detergent containing oxygen or all-fabric bleach.

670 MAKE-UP

Apply dry-cleaning solvent then a weak solution of household detergent to which a few drops of ammonia have been added. Wash as usual.

671 MILDEW

Fabrics may be flushed with diluted bleach from the wrong side. Rinse and launder as normal. Wipe leather with undiluted antiseptic mouthwash. Wipe and rub dry with a soft cloth and then polish.

672 MUD

Allow mud to dry then brush away the excess. Treat any residual stain with dry-cleaning spirit followed by white spirit and then liquid detergent; rinse.

673 NAIL VARNISH

Treat with amyl acetate. Non-oily nail varnish remover or acetone may also be used, though not on acetate fabrics.

674 OIL-BASED PAINT

Treat with turpentine or amyl acetate. Wash as normal.

675 WATER-BASED PAINT

While painting watch for splashes and treat them immediately with cold water. Dried paint becomes permanent.

676 PERFUME

Apply household ammonia straight from the bottle. Rinse thoroughly. Or soak in detergent solution then wash as normal. Any remaining stains may be removed with hydrogen peroxide solution on wet fabric; rinse.

677 PERSPIRATION

Fresh perspiration can be dampened with water then hold the fabric over an open bottle of household ammonia. Sponge old stains with white vinegar. Rinse thoroughly. Stains on wool should be sponged with a 1:1 solution of lemon juice and water. Hang up to air.

678 POLLEN

Clear plastic tape lifts pollen away from fabric. Wash as normal. Some pollen – such as lilies – also needs to be treated with a proprietary stain remover. Check first.

679 RED WINE

Soak excess as soon as possible with water or white wine. Sprinkle with salt before rinsing with cold water or soda water. Wash as normal. If you are particularly prone to spilling red wine, buy a specialist cleaner.

680 RUST

Rusty washing lines or clothes pegs can cause rust stains so be sure to replace them regularly. Soak for 20–30 minutes in a solution made from the juice of 1 lemon combined with one heaped tablespoon of table salt. Rub well, wash and dry. Repeat until the stain disappears.

681 SCORCH MARKS

This stain was traditionally cured with the edge of a bevelled coin. Alternatively, dampen the scorched area with 1 part glycerine to 2 parts water, rubbing the solution in with your fingertips. Soak in 50 g (2 oz) borax to 600 ml (1 pint) of warm water. Leave for 15 minutes and rinse well.

682 SHINY PATCHES

Simmer some ivy leaves in water until tender. Meanwhile brush the garment. Use the resulting liquid to sponge the shiny patches. Brush black clothes with distilled water containing a few drops of liquid ammonia.

683 SHOE POLISH

Treat with dry-cleaning solvent and then a solution of liquid detergent, to which a few drops of household ammonia have been added. Rinse thoroughly. Any remaining stains may be removed with white spirit.

684 SUNSCREEN

Treat with a proprietary grease solvent and then wash as normal.

685 TOBACCO

First flush the stain with cold water. Treat with vinegar and rinse through. If the stain persists, treat it with liquid detergent containing a little methylated spirit. Rinse again.

686 TOMATO KETCHUP/SAUCE

Remove the excess with a spoon and then rinse in cold water. Soak in warm detergent before washing as normal.

687 VEGETABLE OIL (ALSO CASTOR, COOKING & LINSEED OILS)

Apply dry-cleaning solvent several times if necessary. Saturate the fabric in water and treat with white spirit to which a little vinegar has been added. Rinse.

688 WATER SPOTS

Applies especially to silks, rayons and wools. Spritz with water from a water-spraying bottle until just damp. Press while wiping the spot gently with your fingernail.

washing clothes

689 JEAN GENIUS

To preserve the colour of new jeans, wash them inside out. The first wash should be without detergent, too.

690 BEFORE YOU BEGIN

Always separate whites and
colours prior to machine
washing and then arrange
into hot and cool washes;
also hand washes. Empty
pockets, do up zips and
hooks and turn garments
that could fade inside out.

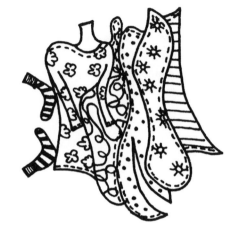

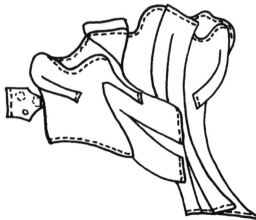

681 LOCK YOUR SOCKS

Invest in some sock lockers (like plastic paperclips) or use safety pins to keep socks together during the wash. You won't have to waste time sorting them into pairs again afterwards.

682 KEEP WHITES RIGHT

Add half a cup of baking soda to the first rinse before you wash your whites, then ¼ cup baking soda to the wash cycle itself. While it may take several rinses to bring out the white, in a hard-water area this will keep your clothes white.

683 LITTLE LIFESAVER

Instead of lugging heavy laundry hampers around the house, place a liner such as a plastic, cloth or mesh laundry bag with a drawstring inside. On laundry day close the bag and throw it downstairs. Return the liner to the hamper.

684 LOOK AT THE LABEL

Though this has been said many times, it is important that you always consult care labels to decide what needs to be hand-washed, dry-cleaned or is machine washable. If you are in any doubt, check with the garment manufacturer. Don't take any chances by ignoring care instructions, if you do you will risk spoiling your favourite clothes.

695 REVITALIZE WHITES

Instead of bleach, try a natural way to revive whites. Unless delicate or synthetic, boil in water with a little soap powder and fresh lemon. Simmer for 10 minutes. The lemon will act as a bleaching agent.

696 PATCHY COLOURS

Chemicals in the water can cause staining and patchy colours, as can some skin creams or powders that come into direct contact with damp, non-colourfast fabric. Re-washing may remove staining but if dyes have been affected, the problem is permanent and the only solution is to re-dye.

697 LOOK AFTER LACE

Make sure lace is machine washable or it may shrink. Prevent snagging by placing it inside a mesh bag or a pillowcase to wash. Or dry-clean or hand-wash in a gentle solution of warm water and a squirt or two of washing-up liquid. Air-dry flat to prevent creasing. Iron in gentle and small circular movements to avoid stretching.

698 LADY IN RED

Prevent brand new red clothes from bleeding over all your other laundry by soaking them in vinegar before the first wash.

699 SHRINKING VIOLET

Washing in too-high temperatures, excessive agitation, tumble drying or direct heat when drying can all cause wool, and even felt, to shrink. Unfortunately the problem is irreversible. Only machine wash if the care label states it is fine to do so. If in doubt, hand wash. Never tumble dry.

700 CHECK THE WEIGHT

Before washing any heavy item, such as a blanket, check the weight against your machine's maximum weights. Avoid squeezing it into the machine – if there's not enough space, it won't rinse or dry properly. You might find it easier to take blankets along to a launderette with commercial size machines especially if you plan to wash several at any one time.

701 SPOTS BEFORE YOUR EYES?

Hard-water deposits present in your local supply can cause white or grey specks. Rewash with the maximum amount of detergent but soak in water softener first. Reduce scale build-up in hard-water areas by doing an 'idle' wash with no detergent and no load.

702 CHECK FIRST

Avoid ruining garments by always using the temperature recommended by the manufacturer on the care label. Use the correct wash programme and avoid over-drying or overloading your machine – all these can cause excessive creasing and perhaps even further damage.

703 COTTON & ACRYLIC CARE

Wash according to the maximum temperature on the care label. To avoid pilling, dry knitted cotton on low heat. A regular setting is suitable for all other cottons. Or hang from a taut clothesline to dry. Acrylics may be tumble-dried on low heat.

704 LAZYBONES

Left your clothes in the machine after a wash? If they are in there for a day or so, especially in hot weather, they will become quite smelly. Rewash with half a cup of ammonia to remove the smell – it works better than laundry detergent.

705 STAIN STRATEGY

However busy you are, don't allow stains to set. If you don't have time to wash clothes immediately, treat them as necessary and leave in a tub to soak.

706 KEEP IT CRISP

Wash table linen before stains start to set. After a big dinner party wash overnight, if possible. Pre-treat stains with commercial cleaner before washing – don't let this dry.

707 WOOL WASH

Pre-treat spots and stains according to the care label. Machine wash on a gentle programme with non-biological powder safe for wool and minimal spin.

708 COLLARS RUCKING?

Collars and the fronts of shirts are stiffened with facings. At different temperatures these shrink, causing puckering of the top fabric. Using cotton thread to repair synthetics also causes puckering as cotton shrinks. Try steam-ironing the still-damp garment and carefully pull offending layers into shape. Wash in cool water to prevent shrinkage or dry-clean special shirts.

709 SOAK YOUR SMALLS

Before you go to bed soak special underwear in a bowl or sink and quickly hand wash in the morning. Tights and under-wired bras especially will last longer if washed this way. Wring tights out properly or they will become longer and longer.

710 WASHING WISDOM

New towels and sheets should be washed together before use. If you wash sets of bedding and towels together at the same regular intervals they will fade equally over time.

711 LAUNDRY LOGIC

Develop a routine that works for you so you keep up-to-date with laundry. Strip beds and replace towels the same day each week. If space allows, separate washing into different baskets so whites are in one, colours another.

712 CREATE A LAUNDRY ROOM

If you don't have a separate utility room, create one from a storage room or large cupboard. Paint it glossy white so it always feels clean. Install a washing machine and tumble dryer with shelves above to store essentials. Hooks on walls or door backs will hold the ironing board and iron.

713 GET THE MOST FROM YOUR WASH

Wash heavily soiled articles alone or pre-wash them by hand. Avoid dealing with stained or heavily soiled laundry for days or stains can set. Do any repairs prior to washing. After the cycle has finished, remove washing and dry quickly to avoid mildew.

714 PURE & SIMPLE

Make sure the water in your washing machine is as pure as possible. Keep the soap drawer clean and to soften the water add soda crystals to your wash. A couple of drops of lavender oil will give your fabric softener a touch of decadence.

carpet & upholstery stains

715 SERIOUS SPILLS

Blot the spill with kitchen paper and gently scrape away as much of the stain as you can. To prevent it from drying out, wrap in plastic. Take the item to a professional cleaner as soon as possible.

716 STAIN ALERT!

First remove as much of the stain as you can by blotting with paper towels (edge to centre) or scrape away with a blunt knife. Avoid rubbing – this pushes the stain into the pile and a circular motion will destroy the texture of the carpet.

717 COFFEE AND TEA

Use a cloth to soak the stain in cold water as soon as possible. Blot with kitchen paper and leave to dry. If the stain persists, soak in hand-hot liquid detergent, rinse and blot dry.

718 POLLEN

If pollen drops onto a carpet gently lift it away from the fabric with sticky tape then use a proprietary stain remover.

719 BLOOD STAINS

Cover a fresh spot with a mix of flour and cold water. Rub gently and dry. Once dried, brush away. Talcum powder also does the trick as does soaking in a little peroxide.

720 CHEWING GUM

Get gum out by rubbing it with peanut butter. Somehow the oil in peanut butter works with the gum to remove it. Peanut butter also removes sticky marks caused by labels.

721 CURRY

Give curry stains on carpets the heave-ho with a solution of diluted lemon juice.

722 EMULSION (LATEX) PAINT

Treat while wet. Rinse in cold water then wash with cold water and laundry detergent. If dry, treat as Make-up/Shoe Polish stains (tip 731).

723 INK

Moisten with a clean white towel and methylated spirits. Gently blot the stain in a clockwise motion (carpet fibres are twisted clockwise). Wait 30 minutes to allow the alcohol to be absorbed. Blot again. Rinse in a solution of one part white vinegar to 10 parts water. Rinse with clean water and a fresh towel.

725 NAIL VARNISH

Blot the excess with a paper towel, then with a cloth moistened with acetone-based nail polish remover. Wipe with a solution of one squirt mild washing-up liquid (without bleach or lanolin) and 1 litre (1¾ pints) of water. Keep blotting as you go. Rinse with clean water and blot again. This works for wooden furniture or floors, too.

724 MUD MARKS

Always leave mud to dry first and then remove as much as possible with a stiff brush. Launder in the cycle recommended for the fabric.

726 GREASE OR OIL

Try sprinkling the area with baking soda to absorb the stain. Vacuum up the excess. Persistent stains may be cleaned in the same way with cornflour.

727 PETS' URINE

Apply baking soda or a solution of three parts vinegar and one tablespoon liquid soap. Leave to work for 15 minutes. Vacuum or rinse off.

728 PROTEIN STAINS

These are baby food, formula milk, cheese and cheese-based foods and eggs. Spray fresh stains with cold water and blot. Repeat until clean. Lightly apply a solution of ¼ teaspoon mild washing-up liquid (without lanolin) in 1 litre (1¾ pints) cold water to dried stains. With a cloth work the solution into the area. Blot with paper towels. Rinse and blot again.

729 RED WINE

To prevent red wine spills from staining, first pour some white wine over the affected area then use a tea towel to mop up the excess (don't rub). Now pour over plenty of salt to leach the stain out of the carpet. When dry, simply vacuum up the salt.

730 BEER SPILLS

To remove beer spills on carpets, simply dab the stain with soda water and a damp sponge.

731 MAKE-UP OR SHOE POLISH

Apply dry-cleaning stain remover. Now rub with liquid detergent and hot water to remove the oil or wax. Launder with laundry detergent and all-fabric bleach. If the stain persists, clean with chlorine bleach.

732 RUST REMOVAL

Try lemon juice and salt. Be sure to test lemon juice on a small area first: some fabrics/carpets may be bleached. If it's OK, sprinkle salt on the stain and squeeze lemon juice over the top. Chlorine bleach makes rust stains permanent.

carpets & rugs

733 DRY CLEANER

Absorb dirt and grease on carpets by sprinkling cornflour over damaged dry areas. Leave for five minutes then vacuum thoroughly.

734 CHECK IT OUT

Before applying commercial cleaner to a whole carpet, test a small area first to see whether the colour will be affected by a wet solution. Never saturate carpet with solution – this encourages mildew and glue deterioration. Decant rinse water and cleaning solution into spray bottles (from garden centres).

735 GO GENTLY

When vacuuming carpets or rugs, use a gentle action – don't scrub – with a regular rather than a rotary head. Work in the direction of the pile only to avoid damaging the surface.

736 MACHINE MAGIC

Use a 3-in-1 cleaner or hire a manual electric shampoo machine or steam cleaner for a more thorough clean. A manual or electric machine dispenses dryfoam shampoo that forms a powder. Dirt is then vacuumed away. A steamer sprays hot water and a cleansing agent under pressure into the carpet then extracts it immediately together with any dirt.

737 RED CARPET TREATMENT

To allow carpets to last as long as possible, avoid walking on them in heavy or high heels. Anything spilt should be swept away or absorbed at once. Grit and dust are damaging to fibres so vacuum at least once a week.

738 NOT-SO-GLORIOUS MUD

Mud can cause havoc on carpets or rugs. Let it dry, then brush ground-in mud to the surface and remove as much as you can with a dull knife. If you still see marks, mix a few drops of washing-up liquid with 200 ml (7 fl oz) warm water. Blot the solution into the area with a clean white towel. Rinse and remove soap residue with another towel.

739 ON THE SPOT

One quick and cheap way to zap spots on rugs and carpets is to use window cleaner. It works just as well as spray-on carpet cleaners.

740 OPTICAL ILLUSION

Choose a dark carpet with very dark, random and non-repeated patterns for a room that will be heavily used. Any stains or dirt will remain hidden. Just don't drop anything dark that you need to find on it!

741 GO OVER GRASS

Vacuum rush as a carpet, lifting occasionally to clean below. Treat stains with a solution of warm water and washing soda. Scrub the surface from time to time with soap and water. Vacuum seagrass often and sponge up any spills. Always check the manufacturer's instructions for sisal and use their recommended cleaning products.

742 PET PONG

If your furry friend is making the room smell, sprinkle baking soda all over the offending carpet or rug. Leave to rest for at least 15 minutes and then vacuum. Another good deodorizer is 250 ml (8 fl oz) cornmeal mixed with 125 ml (4 fl oz) borax. Sprinkle and leave for 15 minutes before vacuuming it up.

743 LIMIT RUG DAMAGE

Rugs respond badly to rapid changes in temperature and humidity. Avoid placing in front of open fires – move with the pile facing outwards to avoid damage.

744 DON'T FADE AWAY

Direct sunlight can cause fading so if your rug or sofa is in a sunny spot, close the curtains at certain times of day.

745 FUR FLYING?

If you have a pet, vacuum at least twice a week especially if anyone in your house suffers from allergies or asthma. Remove excess hair first by wiping over with a damp cloth. If carpets aren't tacked to the floor, vacuum beneath them. Treat upholstery and areas where your pet likes to rest.

746 SIMPLE CARPET SHAMPOO

Mix 125 ml (4 fl oz) washing-up liquid with 500 ml (17 fl oz) of boiling water. Cool – a jelly will form. Use a damp sponge to rub gently into the area. Rinse with a solution of 500 ml (17 fl oz) white vinegar and 1 litre (1¾ pints) of water applied with a clean cloth. Wipe dry with another cloth and repeat as necessary.

747 COIR CARE

Vacuum coir often with a suction-only cylinder vacuum. Mop spills immediately with absorbent paper or a sponge. Wipe over with clean, warm water.

748 HANDLE WITH CARE

Avoid placing delicate or valuable rugs in busy parts of the home. Vacuum gently and slowly with reduced suction in the direction of the pile.

749 SAFE STORAGE

Roll, don't fold rugs and to prevent wearing, roll pile side out. Delicate or antique rugs should be lined with acid-free paper and placed in acid-free boxes to store.

curtains, blinds & shutters

750 AVOID AMMONIA

Aluminium and vinyl blinds don't respond well to ammonia or any other harsh abrasive or cleaner. Instead wash with water and a little washing-up detergent – rinse off afterwards – or try taking them down and washing them in the shower or tub.

751 BADLY SPLATTERED BLINDS

If the drop is longer than the window requires, salvage the blind (if plain or with a non-directional fabric) by detaching the fabric and turning it round. Take the fabric down, unpin from the roller and remove the batten at the base. Cut away the damaged area and tack the new end to the roller. Make a fresh slot for the batten and rehang.

752 THRILL FROU-FROU

Use the upholstery tool to vacuum Austrian and festoon blinds on a low setting. These blinds may require an occasional wash or dry clean.

753 BREAD LINE

You can clean slatted blinds with crusts of fresh bread. Just hold the crusts around each slat as you run them along the length. An old paintbrush will also do the same job or use the brush attachment on your vacuum cleaner.

754 COTTON CARE

Cotton curtains, tablecloths and bedspreads that are exposed to direct sunlight may fade unevenly because the sun will keep moving around during the day. If these items are unavoidably near strong daylight, machine-wash or dry-clean frequently.

755 NEW-LOOK NET

Hand-wash net curtains frequently in hot water but do not exceed recommended temperatures or the fabric will become permanently creased. Rinse in cold water. Whiten with a proprietary cleaner. Re-hang while damp and run a thin rod through the hem until the curtains are dry so they retain their shape.

756 CURTAIN CALL

When slipping curtains over a metal rod, first place a plastic freezer or sandwich bag over the metal end. This avoids snagging the curtains and they will also go on more easily.

757 DUSTY DRAPES

Once a month use the upholstery tool on your vacuum cleaner to remove dust from drapes and pelmets. If the machine is too heavy to lift that high, a feather duster will do the same job. Clean curtains at least once a year according to the care label.

758 PRETTY UP PARCHMENT

Blinds made of natural materials (paper, rice paper or parchment) become damaged by water so clean them with commercial cleaning putty or an art gum eraser.

759 WHAT A WIND-UP

When blinds won't wind, pull halfway down, remove from the brackets and rewind by hand. Pull down and repeat as necessary to re-tension.

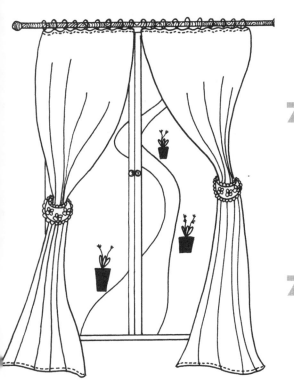

760 PULLING POWER

Avoid skimpy curtains just because fabric is expensive. Instead use two-and-a-half times the width of the window in a cheaper material such as calico, muslin or voile. Ribbons or string threaded with seashells make pretty tiebacks.

761 ROLL UP!

Vacuum rollers with the upholstery tool or use a soft brush. Remove deeper dirt from waterproof blinds by taking them down. To check for waterproofing, sprinkle the surface with a little water – if it sinks, the fabric has not been treated in this way. Sponge with an upholstery shampoo or proprietary blind cleaner and re-hang while damp.

762 TRICK OF THE LIGHT

Bathrooms have blinds made of slightly transparent fabric so they still allow the light in. Heavier material is more suitable for bedrooms where you need to block out the light. Lift the mood in a room with linen blinds in summer and have darker blinds made for winter.

763 WASHING WASHABLES

Remove hooks, weights and loosen heading tape from washable curtains. Shake to remove dust. Soak in cold water, squeeze gently and machine wash on delicates. Iron while damp. Work lengthways on the wrong side, stretching the fabric gently to avoid puckers. Hang while slightly damp (clean tracks, windows and sills first) so they drop to the right length.

764 DO THE MINIMUM

Each month, dust indoor shutters on both sides with the soft brush attachment of your vacuum. In between, touch up with a feather duster. Wear rubber gloves to work with all-purpose cleaner and a spray bottle filled with water to spritz away grime from the slats and crannies. Dry slats one at a time with a cloth.

765 OUTSIDE EDGE

Clean outdoor shutters using the same method as indoor ones (see above) but rinse with a garden hose and as much pressure as your hose can muster. Roughly dry with a towel – the sun will do the rest.

doors, entrances & exteriors

766 BRILLIANT BANISTERS

Dust painted banisters with a soft cloth dampened with a solution of warm soapy water. Rinse section by section and wipe with a dry cloth. Restore moisture to wooden banisters with furniture polish and a soft cloth. Use a cotton bud to clean crevices and tight spaces.

767 CAN'T STOP DOORS CREAKING?

Use a pencil to go over the joins in your hinges. Now work the door back and forth a few times and repeat the process. The graphite in the pencil lubricates the hinges without corroding them. Being dry, graphite won't promote rust.

768 DON'T BE A DOORMAT

If you live in a muddy area, keep a wire rack below your doormat so mud can be scraped from shoes or boots before anyone enters your house. Mats require minimal maintenance: just shake outside to reduce dust and vacuum occasionally.

768 GET INTO GOOD HABITS

Professional painters recommend that you have the outside of your house painted every four years. Schedule the job in before the surface becomes cracked and make sure you choose a reputable decorator through personal recommendation or a professional association.

770 CLEAN SWEEP

Sweep stone steps regularly to remove leaves and twigs or they can stain and become covered in mould. Once a year clean with patio cleaner (from DIY stores) and a stiff-bristled brush. Rinse with a garden hose. Treat stone patios in the same way.

771 PICK A PALETTE

For a display with impact and especially if you have an elaborate container, pick a limited colour scheme such as bold red geraniums with trailing ivy or pastel flowering plants with silver foliage. Save replanting by selecting bedding plants that will last all year round and top up with spring bulbs.

772 ICE BREAKER

When it's freezing outside, mix a solution of warm water and washing-up liquid. Pour it all over steps and they won't refreeze. You can also sprinkle slippery areas with salt.

773 KEEP OFF THE GRASS!

Don't allow your front grass to grow long and then blitz it. In spring and summer remove tips once a week and trim edges regularly. Nourish with feed in springtime when the soil is moist and ideally before rainfall.

774 CHOOSING CONTAINERS

For window boxes, create an impressive display by planting up containers that are similar in style, made from the same material and grouped together.

775 WONDERFUL WINDOW BOXES

All containers require adequate drainage holes and a layer of drainage material such as broken china or large pebbles to prevent compost washing through holes. Pick trailing plants to soften edges, tall ones to add height and some bushy plants to fill in.

776 STOP KEYS STICKING

Work a pencil over the grooves in the key
and gently inside the key hole too. Be
careful: you don't want to break off the tip
of the pencil inside the lock. Work the key
in and out of the lock a few times in a good
'jiggling' motion then gingerly work the lock
with the key.

777 TOP BRASS

Apply non-gel toothpaste (a mild abrasive)
on a soft cloth to door fittings then rub the
brass. Use a fresh cloth to wipe clean. No
further treatment is required for lacquered
brass – otherwise protect with a light
coating of olive or lemon oil.

778 MAKE AN ENTRANCE

Tie a soft old towel over the bristle end
of a broom and brush into all the angles
and crevices of the door where dust
mounts up. Use a soft toothbrush to
tackle detailed moulding. Wash down
with all-purpose cleaner and work
from the bottom up to avoid run marks,
rinsing as you go.

779 MIST OF TIME

Lightly mist wood frames with warm soapy
water and wipe away dirt with a soft cloth.
Wash aluminium annually as wood, rinse
immediately and air-dry. Protect with car wax.

780 KNOBS, HANDLES & KNOCKERS

Mask around fittings with tape and apply
the appropriate cleaning solution. Wipe
glass or ceramic doorknobs with a rag
dampened with methylated spirits.

781 SLIDING DOORS

Vacuum tracks weekly in summer. Wipe with silicone sprayed onto a soft cloth to keep doors sliding smoothly (avoid wood surfaces and the weather strip). Lubricate rollers with light oil. Before washing the door windows, clean the edges of vinyl doors with warm soapy water and rinse with clear water.

fireplaces

782 ANY OLD IRON

Refer to the manufacturer's instructions for your iron fireplace and protect yourself from flaking particles with goggles. Wipe surface dust away with a dry cloth and remove rust from the grate or surround with wire wool. Treat with proprietary remover. Re-blacken with barbecue paint spray (from DIY stores) for a long-term finish. Never clean uncoated iron with water – this encourages rust to form.

783 GRATE IDEA

If you hate cleaning out ashes, spread a wide sheet of aluminium foil beneath fireplace grates – this will catch all the ashes. Once the fire has burned out and cooled, simply fold up around the ashes and remove to your garden for recycling.

784 COLA CLEANER

Try an old masonry trick to brighten up soot-stained brick. Mix a can of cola with 100 ml (3 ½ fl oz) all-purpose household cleaner and 4 litres (7 pints) water in a bucket. Sponge onto sooty brick and leave for 15 minutes. Loosen the soot by scrubbing with a stiff-bristled brush. Sponge with clean water. For a stronger solution, add more cola.

floors & skirting

785 LIGHTEN UP

In dark rooms paint floorboards white to reflect the light and instantly brighten the room. White-painted floors can also be used to enlarge small rooms.

786 TIGHT CORNER

Make the most of all the attachments on your vacuum cleaner (follow the manufacturer's advice). Small tools are perfect for getting into corners or cleaning the top of skirting boards – they get the job done more quickly too.

787 CLEAN SWEEP

Where there's a mix of smooth floors and carpet, choose a cylindrical cleaner to make the job as easy as possible. Pick up any sharp, hard or ungainly objects such as paperclips – these will damage the machine. Run the cleaner over each area at least 12 times in overlapping strokes.

788 CERAMIC CHEER

Remove loose dirt by vacuuming then mop with all-purpose cleaner. Rinse twice with clean water to remove chemicals that could damage the sealant and dry with a clean soft cloth.

789 MARBLE MIRACLES

Never use detergent on marble or the surface will be damaged. Instead try a natural solution of 600 ml (1 pint) white vinegar, 300 ml (½ pint) of water and 20 drops of eucalyptus oil that will keep indefinitely. Pour into a spritzing bottle, shake and pour a little onto a soft, damp cloth. Rub over the surface – there's no need to rinse.

790 SWEEP AWAY

Sweeping is idea for hard-surface flooring such as stone, concrete or wood, but if you have a lot of area to cover, alternate hands to reduce fatigue and play music while you work to make the job pass more quickly.

781 ESSENTIAL FLOOR FRESHENER

Each time you mop the floor, add a few drops of lemon or orange essential oil to the soapy water. It will energize you and leave the room smelling sensational. Lavender oil works beautifully in bedrooms and encourages a restful night.

782 RUBBER SOLES

If your shoes have left black marks all over the floor, try rubbing them out with a pencil eraser. Stubborn marks on hardwood floors can be removed by rubbing with a rag dampened in white spirit. For vinyl floors, smear baby oil over the mark: wait a few minutes and wipe the marks clean away.

783 STAIN REMOVAL WITHOUT SCRATCHING

On laminate flooring, use a dilute solution of vinegar and water to remove stains. Abrasive cleaners, scourers and steel wool will all scratch the floor. Remove shoe polish and other stubborn marks with nail polish remover containing acetone.

784 DON'T BE DULL

To clean laminate flooring, wipe with a damp mop or cloth and avoid over-wetting. Never use soap-based detergents or other polishes as they could leave a dull film on the floor and do not use wax polish.

785 LUSTROUS LINOLEUM

When lino starts to lose its sheen, polish tiles with carnauba wax. Scuffs may be removed with neat turpentine and fine steel wool. Wipe clean with a damp cloth.

786 MEDITERRANEAN MAGIC

To polish floorboards that have been stained but not varnished or painted, apply a little olive oil directly on the wood and dry with a clean cloth. This can also be used on furniture.

787 TIRED TILES

Simply sweep quarry tiles and wash with neutral detergent then rinse in clear water to freshen them up. Do not polish. You can also buy cleaning products from tile outlets. No sealant or polish is required. Restore faded colour with specialist cleaners.

NO SLIP-UPS

Never use soap on stone floors: it cannot be absorbed and makes them slippery. Instead clean with 1 litre (1¾ pints) water to 2 tablespoons washing soda powder.

799 ON THE SLATE

Once installed, protect slate floors from staining by applying stone sealer (gloss or satin). Sealing is especially important in cooking or eating areas. Follow with a protective wax finish – the floor will last longer and be easier to clean. Vacuum weekly and apply a mix of 100 ml (3½ fl oz) ammonia in 6 litres (10½ pints) of water with a sponge mop once a month.

800 VINYL CARE

Sweep vinyl and ceramic floor tiles with a broom. Trapped dirt and sand is highly abrasive and can cause lasting damage to matt and gloss finishes. Avoid using the beater bar of your vacuum – this causes permanent damage. Clean weekly with a damp mop – add a splash of vinegar to the water. Oily or soapy cleaners can leave a dull film.

SHINE ON

Use a soft cloth to apply raw linseed oil to unsealed floors. Allow the oil to sink in, then mop with a little more oil until a shine develops. Sealed wood requires regular sweeping. Wipe occasionally with a damp cloth and wax from time to time to improve the shine.

802 SQUEAKY FLOORBOARDS

Can't stop floorboards creaking? Ease irritating old boards by sprinkling them with French chalk or talcum powder.

803 STOP SCUFFS

To remove scuffs from a vinyl floor, take a rubber-soled shoe such as a tennis shoe and rub the sole across the surface.

804 VARNISH & LACQUER SPRITZ

Mix 2 tablespoons olive oil with 1 tablespoon white vinegar and 1 litre (1¾ pints) water. Transfer to a spray bottle. Spritz floors – and furniture, too – lightly and dry with a damp cloth. Be sure to label the mixture clearly.

805 WHAT A CORKER!

To remove stains from cork without damaging it, scrub a piece of dry bread over the surface. Or pat grimy spots with light masking tape. Clean by wiping with a damp cloth and warm soapy water. Maintain waterproofing qualities by cleaning once a year with specialist liquid wax.

806 WOODY WONDER

Fill a bucket with warm water and add a tablespoon of furniture polish. Clean wooden floors with the solution. The polish will bring out the warm shine of the wood without stripping it of its natural oils.

807 TILE STYLE

Soap makes unglazed and terracotta tiles cloudy. Instead use a 50:50 solution of water and white vinegar. Walls and floors can also be treated with baking soda and a damp sponge. Remove hard-water spots with a soft towel. Finish by polishing with another towel.

hallways & stairs

808 BEAT THAT!

Rugs, kelims, dhurries and doormats attract dust especially in hallways. Every so often hang them over a strong washing line or pole and beat with a broom or carpet beater to keep them in good condition. The energy you expend will keep you in good shape, too.

809 HOOK UP

To prevent hallway clutter, have a row of hooks for bags, baskets, shoes, keys, umbrellas, coats and other paraphernalia. Hanging bags can hide all kinds of junk when visitors are about to descend on you.

810 WELCOME HOME

Place a vase of flowers such as lilies on a table close to the front door to waft scent all over your house and provide an attractive entranceway. You can snip away the stamens to avoid pollen stains but that will spoil the beauty of the flowers so position the vase slightly out of reach where you won't keep brushing against it.

811 MAIL MERGE

Hallways are the place where paperwork can become trapped so resist the temptation to leave letters or bills lying around here. Place them on a metal prong or in a basket or box in your study or office area to deal with.

812 WORK YOUR WAY UP

Avoid grinding dirt into carpets by cleaning stairs from the bottom to the top. After vacuuming the broad stair treads, use a vacuum crevice tool to get into wall cracks and places where the vertical riser meets the tread. From time to time, vacuum the carpet risers.

813 GO EASY

Use a light vacuum and one that's easily manoeuvrable to clean the stairs. Also, it's much easier and safer if you buy an extension lead – avoid trailing leads that could cause accidents, however.

spring cleaning

814 ONCE A YEAR

Look after your attic or loft and you won't encourage dust and mould into your home. A thorough clean once a year is enough – what's more, you'll have a useful storage space.

815 PROTECT YOUR VALUABLES

Protect the floor and your furniture with plenty of large dustsheets (old sheets are perfect). If necessary, secure them over the furniture with low-tack masking tape.

816 BASEMENT BUSTER

Tackle the job wearing a dust mask and rubber gloves. Use a long-handled broom to knock down cobwebs, sweep floors and walls. Wash the floor and walls with hot water and all-purpose cleaner using a strong-bristled floor brush. Rinse in warm water and scrub with household detergent. Afterwards air thoroughly.

817 BRIGHTEN UP BEAMS

Use a lint roller replacement tube attached to a paint roller to run across exposed surfaces. For really dirty beams, climb up on an extension ladder and apply a mix of mild detergent and water with a sponge mop. Just wipe – a damp cloth is all that's required for unfinished beams.

818 STAY SAFE

Always wear a protective mask in basements and lofts and make sure your loft ladder is secure. If you are using equipment such as vacuums, ensure your electrical cord is long enough or use an adequate extension lead.

819 TAKEN TO THE CLEANERS

Before you begin cleaning, take soft furnishings, curtains and bedding to the dry-cleaner. Once you have completed the job, they will be ready.

820 TOP TO TOE

Start at the top of the room and remove light fixtures first. Shades may only need to be dusted or wiped with a damp cloth while chandeliers and other elaborate lighting may have to be taken apart and washed in warm soapy water.

821 SPORT SNEAKERS

Wear trainers to whiz up and down stairs for speedy clean-ups. And wear an iPod or other portable system – you won't waste time changing music.

822 QUICK COVER-UP

Many cleaning products contain strong substances such as abrasives and bleach so always clean in a well-ventilated room. Keep a pair of rubber gloves and protective safety glasses in your cleaning kit.

823 BE PREPARED

Allow at least two days for a big clean. Start early on the first morning and aim to finish the following afternoon to leave the evening free for you to relax. Check you have ample supplies of cleaning products, cloths, sponges and rubbish bags.

824 MAKEOVER MAGIC

In springtime swap heavy drapes at windows for voiles. Consider papering one wall of a room with pretty flowers and butterflies or painting it a lighter shade. Dot vases of hyacinths or narcissi around so you can enjoy their delicious fragrance.

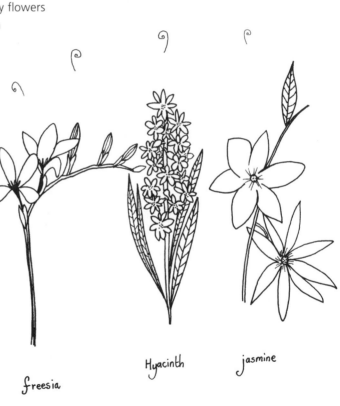

Freesia

Hyacinth

jasmine

825 BALANCE YOUR PH

To remove the fragrance of bleach (and other cleaning materials) from your hands, pour a little vinegar or lemon juice over them and rinse. Bleach is alkaline and vinegar and lemon are acid. Together they cancel each other out and balance the PH of your skin.

826 FILE IT AWAY

Whether it's furnishings or cleaning products, always follow the manufacturer's advice on care. File directions and tips with any new appliance, garment or household item. Unlike guarantees – which should also be filed – these are valid for as long as you have the item. Avoid removing care labels from anything washable.

827 NO SWEAT

Before cleaning, ensure you have ample ventilation. Open all the windows to get fresh air flowing through your rooms, and if your hair is long, tie it back or wear a headscarf, especially if working overhead.

828 SCRUB UP NICELY

Often it's everyday items that shift dirt best. Artists' paintbrushes are perfect for removing fluff from computer keyboards and an old toothbrush scrubs around faucets brilliantly. Nailbrushes can clean showerheads and tackle grout while cocktail sticks or cotton buds are great for teasing dirt out of fine jewellery.

829 ORDER OF PLAY

When cleaning a room, begin with jobs requiring dry methods such as vacuuming, dusting and sweeping. Move on to wet methods with all-purpose and glass cleaner, mopping and so forth. This ensures less dirt will be floating around to cling to wet surfaces.

830 LOOK AFTER NO. 1

Cleaning can play havoc with hands so protect your nails by dabbing petroleum jelly beneath them to keep out dirt. Dot more on cuticles to stop them drying out, roughening or splitting. Wear rubber gloves when dipping your hands into hot water or they will redden and become dry.

VIEW FROM THE TOP

If you're cleaning an entire house, begin at the top and work your way down to avoid trampling dirt into rooms already cleaned. Remove cobwebs from ceilings and covings. Dust light fittings, window frames and wall hangings. Sweep over furniture, skirtings and floors. Start up high with mirrors and windows, too.

TEST FIRST

When using new cleaning products or techniques, experiment with a small, inconspicuous area first so you know whether the object is colourfast or the cleaning method likely to cause damage.

walls & ceilings

CRAYON MARKS

Caught the kids crayoning on their bedroom walls? Dip a damp rag into baking soda and with a little elbow grease the stain will be removed. White spirit can be used on vinyl and gloss but not emulsion (latex) walls.

GRUBBY FINGERMARKS

Look at areas around your home that are at the hand-height of adults or children, such as around door frames, lighting switches and doorknobs and cupboard handles. These areas often get excessively dirty and need extra cleaning.

835 GREASY MARKS ON WALLPAPER

To eliminate grease on wallpaper, first cover the area with blotting or kitchen paper. Apply a warm iron and the paper will absorb the grease.

836 SMUDGES & SPOTS

You can easily remove fingerprints and smudges from wallpaper with an art eraser (from office supply or art and craft stores). Tackle greasy spots with a paste of plain flour and water. Apply and let dry then vacuum up.

837 WASHABLE WALLPAPERS

Wallpaper treated with vinyl is washable but if you're not sure, check first. Wet a hidden area with a tiny solution of a little washing-up liquid and water. If the paper absorbs water, darkens or the colours run, then it's unsuitable for washing.

838 WAX STRIPPER SPRAY

Spray vinyl or rubber coating (cove moulding) with wax stripper spray and allow this to soak for a few minutes to loosen old wax and dirt. Scrub with a nylon brush and rinse.

839 BIT OF A DUST-UP

How often walls need dusting and washing depends on who lives in your house and whether you have a fireplace or wood-burning stove. You can use a lamb's wool duster to freshen up walls or wrap a clean white cloth around a broom – perfect for high-ceilinged rooms.

840 SPOT-CLEAN WITH SODA

Matt and water-based emulsion (latex) walls may be cleaned with a paste made from 4 tablespoons baking soda and 4 tablespoons water mixed together. This removes crayon and ink marks, furniture scuffs and grease spots. Leave for 10 minutes then wipe away with a damp cloth.

841 GO GENTLY

Be gentle on emulsion and stain painted skirtings, dados and casings (framework round windows and doors) – use warm soapy water and a flannel and vacuum regularly with the small brush attachment. Apply the least aggressive cleaner possible to any remaining stains and scuffs.

842 CONTEMPORARY COVER-UPS

Walls today are adorned with all kinds of exciting surfaces including linen, silk, hessian, velvet and some are made of grass, reeds, cork or leather. Generally these are not washable but they respond to gentle cleaning. Vacuum often with the small brush attachment.

843 TRADE SECRET

Professional decorators always start at the bottom of a wall and work their way upward. Apparently dirty water running down a dirty wall leaves worse streaks than dirty water trailing down a clean wall. Apply cleaning solution over a small area, wash in circular strokes, rinse with plain water and wipe dry with a towel.

844 SPRUCE UP SATIN & GLOSS

Clean satin and gloss finishes with a solution made up of 125 ml (4 fl oz) white vinegar, 25 g (1 oz) washing soda and 600 ml (1 pint) water. Or try 200 ml ammonia, 1 teaspoon of washing-up liquid and 4 litres (7 pints) of water mixed together.

845 PERFECT PANELLING

First vacuum dust away with a suitable attachment or remove with a damp cloth unless made of wood. Apply spray-on polish with a soft cloth or for heavier dirt, dampen a cloth with a neutral cleaner. Simulated wood and glossy paint respond well to warm soapy water.

846 WASHING WALLS

Protect floors with a dustsheet. Keep cleaning solution in one bucket, plain water to rinse in another. Avoid marking walls by cleaning with a natural sponge or white cloth. Use a sturdy stepladder or broom to get to tall places.

847 VIEW FROM ABOVE

Wear goggles to protect your eyes while cleaning your ceiling. For a great dusting device, tie a duster onto the end of a long-handled broom. Wipe dirty painted ceilings with a solution of all-purpose cleaner and water plus a damp cloth. Artex and other rough surfaces are best left dry, so vacuum with a soft brush attachment.

848 TWO-IN-ONE PRODUCT

Use solvent – not water – based wood cleaner (from DIY and hardware stores) to clean woodwork, such as dados or skirting, with a shellac or varnish finish. Cleaner and wax in one: apply it with a cloth and buff afterwards.

849 GREASE IS THE WORD

Methlyated spirits cuts through grease on real wood panelling with a penetrating finish but work quickly and reapply, or touch up oil or stain finishes afterwards.

850 REDUCE DAMAGE

While the kids may be kicking the skirtings, it's more likely to be your vacuum cleaner that's doing the most damage. Check the bump in front is in place and avoid mopping the floor with a mop with a sharp swivelled head.

851 INSTANT SPACE

To brighten up any room and make the space seem larger, try an old trick favoured by those in the property trade. Simply apply a coat of white paint to a clean ceiling.

852 WHITER SHADE OF PALE

Clean vinyl-coated ceiling tiles with a solution of 15 ml (½ fl oz) hydrogen peroxide (mild bleach) and 500 ml (17 fl oz) water shaken together in a spray bottle. Spray evenly over the tiles and air-dry. Freshen up non-coated tiles by wiping with a just-damp cloth.

853 SCUFFED SKIRTINGS

Gloss paint skirtings to make them easy to clean and hard-wearing. Remove scuffs and dirt with a sponge and grease-cutting all-purpose spray cleaner. Treat tough stains with scouring powder and a plastic scrubbing pad.

854 VACUUMING VENTS

Floors, walls and ceilings often have angled louvre vents that are designed to ventilate the house while preventing dust and debris getting in. They do collect dust, however, and need regular vacuuming with the brush attachment to loosen dirt. Twice a year detach and clean both sides or wipe with a moist dust cloth.

855 DON'T BE A STREAKER!

Streaking on walls, glass and other surfaces is often caused by spraying a cleansing agent directly onto the surface and then using a cloth. To avoid this, always spray onto a cloth and then use the cloth to clean.

windows

856 BEGIN AT THE BEGINNING

Clean window frames and sills before you start to clean the glass. Vacuum to remove any loose dirt and then wipe down with a damp cloth.

857 GLEAMING GLASS

For glass that stays clean and static-free, add one tablespoon of cornflour to about 1.2 litres (2 pints) of lukewarm water. Wet a rag, squeeze away excess water and wipe down the glass. Because the rag is less static, dust and debris build up less frequently.

858 SPOTLESS SASHES

Take care at all times when cleaning sashes – no major leaning out is necessary to do this well. The most efficient method is to clean from the outside top down to the bottom part of the inside window working the sashes as you go.

859 KEEP PLASTIC PRISTINE

Avoid using cleaner containing ammonia on plastic windows – it leaves the surface permanently cloudy. Instead, use a handful of pure soapflakes mixed with one tablespoon washing soda and 600 ml (1 pint) water.

860 BE A PROFESSIONAL

The squeegee is the window cleaner's number one choice. Select one with a replaceable rubber blade. Technique is very important – draw the wet squeegee across the top of the pane, keep drawing it down one side of the glass until it's almost at the bottom. Repeat, working across with overlapping strokes, and wiping in between.

861 LOVELY LOUVRES

Mix 200 ml (7 fl oz) vinegar in 3 litres (5¼ pints) water. Open the window to its fullest extent so that the slats are perpendicular with the window frame. Dip a thick white cotton sock in the solution, wring and place over your hand like a mitten. Starting at the top, clean the slats on both sides. Use a clean dry sock to dry in the same manner.

862 COBWEB CATCHER

Use a long-handled, clean, barely-damp mop to catch and remove dust and cobwebs easily and effectively from tall windows and skylights.

863 LOOKING AFTER ALUMINIUM

Window and door frames made of aluminium have a tough coating, but this can be scratched by abrasive cleaners so use a smooth cloth and a bowl of hot water and washing-up liquid to clean them. Afterwards dry thoroughly.

864 PRESERVE FRAMES

If you can reach them, clean the frames of skylights with furniture polish. Finish, paint or stain them every three years to keep the wood in good condition and protect it from ultraviolet ray damage.

865 PROTECT PANELS

Clean wood louvres with an oil finish. Dampen a cloth with boiled linseed oil, mineral spirits or turpentine (from hardware and paint stores).

866 REACH FOR THE SKY

Preserve your view by cleaning skylight exteriors twice a year. More often and you may wear out the silicone seal around the edge and cause leaks. Clean inside monthly with a long-handled squeegee and commercial window cleaner.

867 SMEAR-FREE FINISHES

Keep a supply of white vinegar in the house. It's truly indispensable when it comes to cleaning glass and windows. Add to warm water and a little detergent plus a bit of baking soda. Scrunched-up balls of newspaper add extra glossy sheen when it comes to the final buff.

868 WATCH OUT WITH LEADING

Leaded and stained glass window require extra care. Wash the panes individually with plain, warm water and a clean cloth. Make sure you don't use too much force or you can actually bend them. Never wash with household glass cleaners, vinegar, lemon, ammonia or anything with an abrasive action.

869 SPOT STREAKS

Clean one side of the
window with up-and-down
strokes, then work from side to
side on the other. This makes it
easy to notice and remove streaks.

870 SUN, SUN, SUN

You may think lovely weather makes
a good day to tackle outdoor cleaning,
but strong sunlight can cause window
cleaner to dry before you can work it
off – this may cause streaks. See which
way the sun is moving around your
house and work accordingly.

871 TALL ORDER

Use a spongy floor mop to get to the
high-up and hard-to-reach windows.
You may even need to open one
window and lean out to clean
another. But don't take risks:
hire a professional cleaner to
do the more difficult windows
and save money by cleaning
the more accessible ones.

first aid

872 ANIMAL BITES

Wash the wound with soapy water. Rinse, dab dry and apply a clean dry dressing. If it is large or deep, go to the Emergency department of your local hospital and check you are covered for tetanus. Report dog bites to the police – rabies is potentially fatal.

873 ASTHMA ATTACK

Call emergency services if the patient is having an asthma attack that is more severe than normal, if the attack is not relieved by usual medication (such as inhalers) or if it is a first attack.

874 BLEEDING

Raise the wound and apply pressure to the bleeding point with a clean cloth pad. Apply a dressing and bandage. If blood seeps through, place another bandage on top (do not remove the first). If it continues to seep through, remove both bandages and reapply, exerting pressure on the bleeding area. Seek medical help.

875 BROKEN BONES

Signs of a broken bone include distortion, swelling and bruising; also pain and difficulty moving the injured part. The patient should be taken to the nearest hospital emergency department.

876 BURNS & SCALDS

First cool the affected area by holding it under cold running water, immersing in water or pouring cold water over it for at least 10 minutes or until the pain subsides. Apply a sterile dressing and bandage. Do not use ointment, sticking plaster (bandaids) or treat the burn with cotton wool or fluffy material.

877 NOSEBLEEDS

Have the person sit down and lean forward. Ask them to breathe through their mouth and squeeze the soft part of their nose for at least 10 minutes. Reassure and help them if necessary. Go to the hospital if the nosebleed is severe or lasts more than 30 minutes; also if the patient suffers persistent nosebleeds.

878 CUTS & GRAZES

Clean grit and dirt away with running water. Dab dry and apply a sterile dressing (do not use ointments or creams). Ask when the person was last immunized for tetanus and consult a doctor if necessary for a booster shot; also if the cut is sore and inflamed or oozes pus. Go to the hospital if the wound is deep.

879 ELECTRIC SHOCK

Study the casualty first: don't touch them or the shock could be transferred. Check that the power is off. Once you are sure they are away from the electricity source, check their circulation and breathing. Resuscitation may be required. Call emergency services.

880 FAINTING

Encourage the patient to lie down flat if not already on the ground. Make sure plenty of fresh air is circulating – open windows if necessary. Kneel down in front of them. Support their raised legs by placing their ankles on your shoulders.

881 SPLINTERS

Clean the area with soap and water. Sterilize a pair of tweezers (pass through a flame from a match or lighter); then cool. Do not touch the ends of the tweezers or wipe away any soot. Hold the tweezers close to the skin, without actually touching it. Now grip the end of the splinter and pull it out. Squeeze the wound to encourage a little bleeding. Clean and dry the area; apply an adhesive dressing. If the splinter breaks, consult your doctor or local hospital.

882 BEE & WASP STINGS

If the sting remains in the skin, brush or scrape it off with a fingernail or blunt knife (do not use tweezers). Never squeeze the skin or you could spread the insect's venom. Apply a cold compress or ice pack to relieve pain and reduce swelling.

883 POISONING OR OVERDOSE

Try not to panic and call the emergency services immediately. Try to find out what the patient has swallowed and take the remains (empty bottle, etc) to the hospital with them. Resuscitation may be required if the patient collapses.

884 RASH

If a rash does not fade when a glass is pressed to it, meningitis may be indicated. Watch out for other symptoms, which may include high temperature, vomiting, severe headache, neck stiffness, joint or muscle pains, confusion, drowsiness, a dislike of bright lights and seizures. Call the emergency services immediately.

885 SUNBURN & WINDBURN

Cover the burnt skin with light clothing or a towel. Move the patient to the shade. Sponge the affected area with cold water and give the casualty sips of water. Do not break any blisters. Apply calamine lotion to mild burns, but if burns are severe, get medical aid.

886 STINGS & ITCHING

Light rashes such as nettle stings or poison ivy may be treated with calamine lotion. Washing and cleaning products can irritate your skin so if in doubt, change them. If problems persist, consult your doctor.

natural home remedies

887 BEAT WASP & BEE STINGS

Slice an onion in half and rub the cut side over a bee or wasp sting to ease the pain.

888 CATNIP REPELLENT

For an effective insect repellent, rub fresh catnip leaves over the exposed skin or use extract of catnip.

889 COLD CURE

Finely chop a few garlic cloves, cover with honey and leave for two to three hours. Take teaspoons throughout the day.

890 MORNING OR TRAVEL SICKNESS

Ginger will soothe the digestive system and is safe to take during pregnancy. Drink ginger tea or chew a little piece of the root.

891 HELP FOR HANGOVERS

Eat two apples as soon as you wake up. This will replace lost vitamins and reduce the effects of dehydration.

892 INSECT BITES & STINGS

Rub neat lavender essential oil directly onto the sting or mix up a paste of 1 teaspoon baking soda and a little water or vinegar. Apply directly to the sting.

893 NATURAL PAINKILLER

Blend three small de-seeded chillies with 600 ml (1 pint) tomato juice and a dash of soy sauce. Drink as much as you can to release endorphins into the body.

894 TOOTHACHE

Place 1–2 drops of essential oil of cloves on cotton wool and dab onto the sore area. If problems persist, consult your dentist.

895 RELIEVE HEADACHES

To ease tension from headaches, mix two tablespoons ground ginger with a little water; warm gently in a saucepan. Spread the mixture onto a lint pad to make a poultice. Lie down in a dark and quiet room with the pad pressed on your forehead.

896 SMALL CUTS & WOUNDS

Apply neat lavender essential oil to burns or cuts to help them heal quickly. This also helps prevent scarring. Keep small cuts clean and germ-free with the cut side of a piece of garlic or onion.

897 SORE THROAT

Mix hot fresh lemon juice together with a teaspoon or two of honey for one of the oldest and best remedies for a sore throat.

898 TUMMY TROUBLE

Try a cup of black tea or drink fresh lemon or a little lime juice mixed with water to ease stomach ache. Treat indigestion or heartburn with two teaspoons of bicarbonate of soda mixed with 50 ml (1¾ fl oz) water.

pest control

899 BAG BAIT

If you're squeamish, place a brown paper lunch bag around a baited mousetrap. The mice seem drawn to exploring a small space and all you have to do is close the bag and dispose of it once they've been caught.

900 GIVE FLIES THE BRUSH-OFF

If you prefer not to use chemical fly spray and fly-swatting fills you with horror, invest in a fan. Scientists say that flies' wings are unable to operate in a breeze above 15 km (9 miles) an hour. Open the windows, turn the fan to full power and they'll soon buzz off.

901 BEAT BEDBUGS

Found in murky mattresses, behind window frames and plastic cracks, among other places, these lice-like insects appear at night to prey on you. Although there are solutions you can try at home such as smearing petroleum jelly on legs of beds to prevent them crawling up, it's better to call in your local pest control.

902 CAMPING OUT WITH COCKROACHES?

These big black beetles appear at night to eat food, starch, fabrics and paper. Sprinkle infested areas with pyrethrum paper. If problems persist, call your local pest control officer.

903 CARPET EATERS

If you spot carpet beetles, act quickly by contacting your local pest control. These insects will be looking for fabric in which to lay their eggs. As larvae hatch, they will eat through their surroundings and can cause widespread damage.

904 HOPPING MAD

If you have fleas in the house, vacuum all carpets and rugs, concentrating on areas frequented by your pet, especially beneath seats and sofas. Also vacuum upholstered furniture, then empty and throw away the bag. Wash bedding and removable rugs. Using a spray bottle, apply specialist flea-killing product. Treat your pet with flea powder or capsules recommended by the vet at the same time.

905 CHALK IT UP

Plagued with ants? They are said
never to cross a chalk line so get your
chalk out and draw a line on the floor
or wherever they tend to march.
For some reason ants also
dislike cinnamon so place
it wherever you have
noticed them.

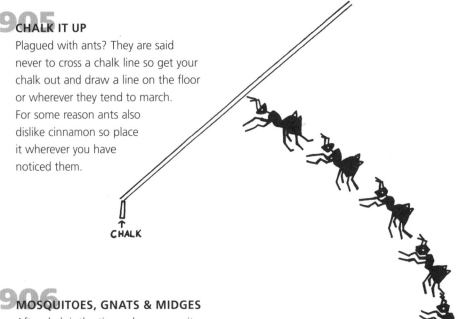

CHALK

906 MOSQUITOES, GNATS & MIDGES

After dark is the time when mosquitoes cause
the most trouble, so wear insect repellent
and cover your arms and ankles. Cover water
butts and keep drains and gutters clear; also
renew water in birdbaths to avoid attracting
these creatures. Repel mosquitoes by adding
a few drops of citronella oil to a saucer of
water, fitting screens to windows and using
impregnated coils.

907 FRIENDLY CRITTERS

Spiders will eat flies and other unfriendly
insects in the home. What's more, they are
completely harmless. Sweep cobwebs away
with a clean broom or feather duster.

908 CHOOSE CITRONELLA

Indoors and out, in hot weather light a few citronella scented candles to deter mosquitoes and other midges. Nightlights and special garden candles are available to ensure eating al fresco is an enjoyable experience.

909 FLY AWAY

Flies can spread at least 30 different diseases to animals and humans so prevent them by keeping food and garbage tightly covered and dustbins clean. Mint, basil and strongly scented marigolds are also thought to deter them.

910 MAKE MICE DISAPPEAR

Buy a standard snap-back trap (from hardware stores). Bait with peanut butter, oatmeal or cheese. You can also use cotton wool – mice enjoy making nests out of it. Avoid poison: it can be harmful to pets and dead mice may be left out of reach where they can attract other household pests. When baiting wear gloves – mice have an acute sense of smell.

911 HIRED HELP

If you have an aquarium, certain species can help with the cleaning by gobbling up algae. Freshwater bristlenose or saltwater turbo snails will be happy to shift the dirt. Just be sure they're compatible with other creatures in your tank. Obtain professional advice before keeping any fish – for them, cleaning can be a life-or-death matter!

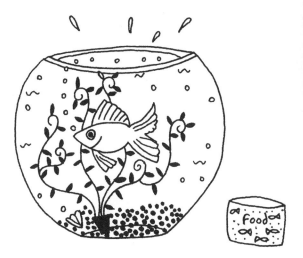

203

912 COLLECT CONKERS

To prevent moths, place conkers (horse chestnuts) in cupboards and closets. They are easy to find and won't cost you a penny. Store out-of-season clothes in airtight bags or plastic containers to help.

913 STOP STRAYS

Prevent stray cats coming through your cat-flap by fitting an electromagnetic cat flap (from pet stores). This comes with two magnets: one in the cat flap and the other goes on your cat's collar to activate the lock.

914 MUNCHING WEEVILS

Weevils arrive in your home in packets of food. Although harmless, they will go on to destroy other food in the same cupboard and you can see them in certain foods such as whole-grain cereals and pasta. Throw away affected food and other opened packets – place it in a secure bag and put it in the outside waste bin at once. Empty the cupboard and then wash and dry before refilling.

915 NASTY NITS

If the kids are scratching and you spot tiny white egg sacs attached to their hair, you know you've got lice in the house. Ask your local pharmacist about head lice treatments and alert families of friends who play with your children. In severe cases natural pesticides such as quassia, neem oil or tea tree oil can also be used.

916 PRACTICAL PERFUME

Camphor bricks or lavender bags will keep moths at bay. In addition, they leave everything in your cupboard smelling delicious. In time their smell fades, so change them once a year. Essential oils such as cedar, eucalyptus and lavender dabbed on handkerchief or pieces of cotton and stored with your clothes will do the same job.

917 KEEP A CAT

Avoid mice by keeping a cat – often just the smell of a cat is enough to drive them away. Keeping all food in tightly sealed jars and tins and garbage tightly covered are other deterrents.

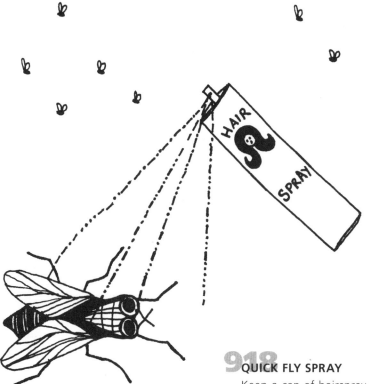

918 QUICK FLY SPRAY

Keep a can of hairspray to hand – it's ideal for zapping flies when you don't have fly spray. Flypapers are also effective and won't harm the environment.

919 READ ALL ABOUT IT

If you have a problem with earwigs, just roll up a newspaper and leave it in the area overnight. When you wake up the next day, the earwigs will be inside the paper. Put it in a plastic bag and throw it away.

920 REMOVING RATS

Rats are attracted to anywhere food has been left out including open garbage cans and compost heaps. Old rags encourage them to create a cosy nest. While you can deal with the occasional rat with poisoned bait (keep pets and children away), it's far better to hire a professional immediately.

921 SERIAL STINGERS

Unlike bees, wasps can sting again and again. If you spot wasps flying to one spot, look for a nest – which can produce up to 30,000 wasps. Contact your local health authority to remove it without delay. For small numbers, fill a jar with half jam and half water. Cover with paper punctured with holes to attract, trap and drown them.

922 SILVERFISH DETERRENT

Troubled with silverfish? Try placing whole cloves in closets and drawers. Or sprinkle Epsom salts at the back of cupboards.

923 WORRIED ABOUT WOODWORM?

If pinhead holes with sawdust spilling out appear in woodwork or furniture, call in the professionals immediately. Otherwise woodworm will make themselves at home and quickly bore into wooden furniture, beams and floorboards.

pet problems

924 ACCIDENTS WILL HAPPEN

Brace yourself and pick up as much pet poo or vomit as you can with paper towels – flush this away in the lavatory. Now apply a specialist cleaner with active enzymes designed to deal with pet mess. Rinse with water to avoid leaving smells that could entice your pet to use the same spot again.

925 BEDTIME FOR BONZO

Choose washable bedding for your pet and wash frequently at 60 °C (140 °F) to kill bugs and eggs from fleas. Tumble-drying sterilizes and removes stray hairs. If you allow your pet on your own bed or furniture, protect it with a removable cover and wash the covers below regularly.

926 PREVENT HUMAN ALLERGIES

A special cleansing liquid is now available on the market that removes Fel d1 and dander – the prime causes of allergic reactions to cats and small animals. Just groom your pet to remove any dead hair and moisten a soft cloth with the clear treatment. Apply all over your animal, rubbing the coat both with and against the hair. Repeat every seven days.

927 PARCEL FORCE

If you have pets, keep plenty of parcel or masking tape in the house. It's perfect for removing pet hair, especially if you have a long-haired cat or one that moults a lot.

928 GOOD GROOMING

Regular combing of your pet removes dead skin and saliva flakes that cause allergies in humans; it also makes your pet less smelly. If possible, groom outdoors so hairs and flakes get blown away rather than redistributed in the home.

929 FLEA PREVENTION

Every day add one garlic capsule to your pet's food. This helps prevent roundworm and also deters fleas.

930 HYGIENE HABITS

Be sure to vacuum and mop regularly around and beneath pet beds as well as their favourite places around the home. Blot up urine as soon as you spot it. Rinse area in vinegar solution, blot and dry.

931 PET CARE

If you've taken on the responsibility of keeping an animal, make sure their immunizations are kept up to date and it pays to take out adequate pet insurance so they can enjoy the best possible care.

932 PONGY PETS

If you have pets, avoid distinctly doggy or clearly catty smells in the home by keeping up good grooming and rigorous cleaning routines. Make sure the place is well ventilated and use natural products to scent or deodorize to avoid harming your furry friends.

933 QUICK PICK-UP

To remove animal hair from fabric or carpets, try this miraculous trick. Drag a damp sponge in small bursts over the surface. The hairs will stick to the moist sponge and leave the area hair-free. Rinse the sponge frequently.

934 WHEN TO GET THE VET

It's always best to consult your vet if you suspect your pet has fleas or worms. Follow the directions on any products carefully and don't assume that the treatment you use for your dog will work equally well on a cat. If you are unlucky enough to experience an infestation of fleas, call on expert help to treat the problem efficiently and safely before it becomes widespread.

professional services

935 AVOID COWBOYS

Never have a job done by someone who happens to be 'in your area'. Shop around to avoid 'special prices', which might be high for that kind of work. Check out tradesman before you hire them – seek references from at least one other householder.

936 KEEPING YOUR CLEANER

Good cleaners are in demand so be kind to yours and pay him or her promptly. Establish proper boundaries and keep your relationship professional – if you've shared your innermost secrets, it will be hard to complain when the windows are covered in smears.

937 SEEK COMPANY PREMISES

Be wary of tradesman you can contact only by phone – if things go wrong they might be hard to find if they don't have a registered address. Don't suffer in silence: report problems to trading organizations.

938 PERFECT TREASURE

Cleaning doesn't come naturally to everyone, especially if you are seeking work-life balance. Consider hiring someone to do the job for you – ideally through personal recommendation; you are handing over your door keys so trust is imperative.

939 SPRING INTO SPRING

If you want professional cleaning without the cost of a regular cleaner, pay a cleaning company to spring clean your home. Have a top-to-toe clean throughout or just concentrate on carpets and curtains for quick and dramatic results.

940 TAKE A TOUR

Walk a new cleaner round your home and agree a basic set of tasks and time scale. Jobs can change from week to week so establish some flexibility. Explain security and alarm systems. Check they know how to care for any valuables or designate the job to yourself. It's polite to tidy up before they arrive, but don't feel you have to clean.

941 CHECK ESTIMATES

Be wary of late estimates and be sure to get estimates on company letterhead with a detailed breakdown of costs plus taxes. Check how long the job will take and whether materials are included. Will the firm agree a fixed price before beginning the work? When are deposits and stage payments due? Is the tradesman easy to get hold of and happy to answer questions? Get everything in writing.

quick fixes

942 DRIPPING OVERFLOW

A faulty float or ball valve can't control the flow of water from the tank to the lavatory cistern so water drips through the overflow pipe. For a temporary fix, tie the float arm to a piece of wood laid across the top of the cistern – while in place, you won't be able to flush the toilet. For a permanent repair, call a plumber to repair or replace the ball float.

943 BREAKFAST IN BED

Mop up stains and spills on duvets or quilts at once to avoid soaking through the filling. If the casing is stained, ease the filling away from that area. Tie off with an elastic band or string. Sponge first with cold water and then go over the area with mild detergent.

944 BRILLIANT BICARB

Coat stubborn stains on laminated furniture with a paste of bicarbonate of soda. Leave for several hours and then rub briskly before wiping off. Toothpaste also does the same trick.

945 GET OUT OF A TANGLE

For horrible tangles in thin necklaces or bracelets, place on a glass surface. Add a drop of baby oil and use a pin to tease out the knots. Rinse in warm water.

946 MILK BATH

To remove hairline cracks in china, soak it overnight in a bowl of warm milk. Gently hand-wash as normal and you'll find the crazed lines will have disappeared.

947 BROKEN GLASS

A pad of damp cotton wool is perfect for picking up tiny fragments of broken glass. Dab the affected area and the glass will stick to the pad, which can then be thrown away.

948 GOOD-AS-NEW PORCELAIN

Disguise chips and scratches on white porcelain with white enamel paint. Following the package instructions, paint over the mark with a small artist's brush. Dry, rub with fine sandpaper and repaint. Repeat until the area matches the surrounding surface.

949 HANGING HEAVY PICTURES & MIRRORS

Use glass plate hooks, which need to be screwed to the wall and frame, instead of weak metal picture hooks. For wooden frames use a normal screw; a self-tapping screw grips better on metal or mirror frames. Screw the glass plate hooks into the frame, then drill holes, fit rawlplugs and screw to the wall.

950 STOPPER UNBLOCKER

If the stopper is stuck in your decanter or any other glass bottle, put on rubber gloves to protect your hands and enhance your grip. Wrap a hot, damp cloth around the neck of the decanter to expand the glass, then slowly dribble vegetable oil round the stopper. Gently wiggle and twist the stopper to work it free.

951 GRASS STAINS ON SPORTSGEAR

Rub a bar of ordinary soap directly onto the stain to remove it. Use plenty of elbow grease and you'll find the stain disappears quickly – it's also cheaper than expensive stain removers.

952 LEAKY WINDOWS

A wooden window sill should have a drip groove underneath it to allow rainwater to run away from the house. If this is missing, paint or stain a fillet of wood to match the sill. Nail it to the underside, near the front, to keep water away from the wall.

953 STEPPED IN TAR?

If you have managed to walk into some tar, remove as much of it as possible by scraping it away gently with an old spoon, then blot up with paper towels. Dampen a wad of paper towels with methylated spirits and apply. Repeat as necessary. Treat any remaining tar with a mix of warm water and washing-up liquid. Spray with clean water to rinse and wipe dry.

954 LIFT COLLARS & CUFFS

Give a grubby shirt (or blouse) a boost by brightening up tired collars and cuffs with a dab of shampoo. Keep some shampoo in your office drawer to limit the damage caused by journeying on subways or tubes.

955 POT POURRI PAST ITS BEST?

Bring back potpourri that's looking a little tired by placing it in a microwave proof bowl and heating it for 10 seconds.

956 MAYO MARVEL

White rings caused by water or heat on furniture may be removed with a paste of mayonnaise and cigarette ash. Leave for an hour or so, remove the paste and buff up with a damp cloth. This also works on cigarette burns.

957 SHOE SHINE

You can quickly smarten up shoes by cleaning them with baby wipes. Over time this technique will dry out leather, so only use it when you're in a hurry – follow up with polish later on.

958 SURFACE SCRATCHES

Remove scratches on glass by rubbing a little toothpaste onto the surface. Finish by polishing with a soft cloth.

959 TARNISHED TEAPOTS

Use a proprietary silver dip to remove tarnishing, water scale and tea stains from silver teapots. Pour the contents of the dip inside the teapot and swirl around. Rinse well before using.

960 WAX WORKS

If your favourite vase is leaking, coat the inside with a thick layer of paraffin wax and leave to dry. For china, apply porcelain enamel over the cracked area with a small brush or make-up brush until the crack is filled. Allow to dry for 24 hours.

961 WOBBLING CHAIRS

Level annoying uneven legs on chairs by cutting them to the length of the shortest leg. You can also build up the short leg to match the rest. Glue and screw the extra piece in place so the chair is perfectly stable.

safety & security

962 LEAKING GAS

Never ignore the smell of gas – it is always a warning. Learn where the gas mains are located in your house and how to close the valve in case of a leak. If you can smell gas, contact your supplier immediately – never use an open flame to look for a gas leak.

963 BURGLAR DETERRENTS

Don't let people see inside your home as this is a good way to spot anything worth stealing; draw curtains or blinds whenever you put the lights on. If you are selling your home, have the estate agent call you about every viewer and make sure they accompany potential purchasers.

964 WELL-LIT SPACES

You'll feel safer if you can see who is at your door. Have enough light outside your front door and fit a peephole to a door or window so you can see without being seen.

965 TAKE ACTION

Until a gas leak is found and repaired, evacuate family, friends and any pets from your house. Open all doors and windows and check the boiler pilot light is out. Do not smoke, use a naked flame or turn the electricity on or off in the vicinity. Once the leak has been repaired, make sure all pilot lights are re-lit.

966 UNDER LOCK AND KEY

Lock the doors and windows when you go out, even if it's just for a few minutes. When you go to bed, lock up, but keep keys accessible for emergencies.

967 KEEP A GOOD SUPPLY

Power failures are never convenient but being without electricity after dark can be unnerving, too. Have a stock of emergency items in case of a power failure – a working torch (flashlight), spare batteries, candles and matches in one or more accessible locations. Buy a battery-operated radio so you can check local news while the power is down.

968 DON'T LET THEM IN

Keep the door on the chain while you get a caller's ID. Never invite salespeople inside. Ask for a brochure or card and say you need to talk to someone else. Never hand over cash and don't be taken in by someone offering to do repairs.

969 UTILITY COMPANIES

Make sure they have an appointment and ask to see their photo ID. If they have forgotten it, ask them to go back and get it. Check they know the name and account number on your bills and wait for them to tell you what job they have come to do. If in doubt, check with their office – genuine workers won't mind waiting or coming back.

970 HIGH & DRY

Keep medicines in a cool, dry place – heat and humidity can affect potency so a steamy bathroom is not ideal. Store on high shelves in cupboards or a dedicated cabinet out of sight and reach of children. Anything beyond the expiry date should be thrown away.

971 CIRCUITS & FUSES

Learn the location of your fuse box and how to repair a fuse. Keep one or two spare fuses to hand. If you have a circuit breaker, label all switches and know how to turn them off.

972 ASK A FRIEND

Have a friend or neighbour check the inside of the house for you while you are away on holiday in case of any emergencies. Make sure they have your contact number and a list of emergency contacts.

973 STOP THE POST

Either get your mail temporarily stopped while you are on holiday or have a friend take in your mail – post left sticking out of the letterbox could entice burglars.

974 DEEP-FAT DRAMA

Avoid filling a deep-fat fryer so the oil is more than a third of the way up the pan. If fat catches fire while you are cooking meat, sprinkle both the fat and the meat with bicarbonate of soda to put out the flames.

975 BE NEIGHBOURLY

Avoid being locked out by leaving a spare set of keys to your house with someone local that you can trust. Return the favour and keep a set of their keys, too. Have a sense of community – it's good to have neighbours you can turn to in an emergency even if you don't want to live in each other's pockets. Neighbourhood Watch schemes are known to prevent burglaries and membership may even lower your household insurance.

976 EMERGENCY RATIONS

Keep a storage shelf full of all the items you regularly need to keep your home in order and running smoothly. These could include light bulbs and batteries, clear adhesive tape and scissors, string, spare plugs, a set of screwdrivers, extra-strong glue, a jar containing a small amount of cash for emergencies, stationery and stamps; also jars of spare nails, screws and safety pins. Replace any supplies as you use them.

977 PROTECT YOUR PRIVACY

Your phone company can help and advise on how to trace callers and remove your number from directories. Keep your personal details private. Put only your last name on a doorbell or nameplate or ID badge at work.

978 FIRST AID BOX

Keep a first aid kit. Every home should have the following – porous surgical tape, large and medium wound dressings, sterilized cotton wool, tubular gauze bandages, large triangular bandages, a standard crepe bandage, tweezers, an eye bath, a sharp sterilized needle, safety pins, plasters (bandaids) of all sizes and sharp scissors.

979 LEAVE A LIST

On your kitchen notice board or anywhere else that's prominent, keep a list of useful numbers (plumber, electrician, utilities companies, doctor, dentist, and so on) so you always have these easily to hand. Make sure everyone in your house knows where the list is located and update it as necessary.

980 REGISTER WITH A DOCTOR

Make sure you and your partner or family are registered with a local doctor. Choose one through personal recommendation if you can. You may have to make an initial appointment to go on their books. Do the same with a local dentist.

981 CHECK IT OUT

Every week test the batteries in your smoke alarm. Light a match beside it and blow it out. The smoke should activate the alarm. If activated by light, set it off by shining a flashlight into the alarm. Pressing the button on the casing is not enough of a test – it only indicates the horn is working, not the detection mechanism.

982 SMOKE ALARM MAINTENANCE

Vacuum your smoke alarm every other month – cobwebs, dust and spiders can cause the alarm to become less sensitive and work less effectively. Cover the alarm when doing major work around the house that could send dust into the air or while painting. Uncover again promptly once you've finished.

983 TOO HOT TO HANDLE

However lazy you might be feeling, never use a damp or wet teacloth to handle anything hot in the kitchen. The water will transmit the heat through the cloth and burn your hands.

984 NOISY NEIGHBOURS

First approach your neighbours about the noise problem. Explain how the noise is affecting you – even ask them to come and listen to it from your home. If they are unhelpful, contact your local environmental health department. They will investigate your complaint and take legal action if they decide the noise is a nuisance.

985 OVERHANGING TREES

If a neighbour's tree overhangs your garden, you can ask them to trim it back. If they refuse, you have the right to trim back to the boundary line. Though it sounds odd, your neighbour owns any branches or fruit removed so offer to return them. Before trimming any tree, check in case it is protected by a preservation order.

986 LOOK AFTER YOUR PASSWORD

If someone finds out your password, they can charge their Internet use to your phone bill. If you suspect this might be the case, change your password the next time you sign on and let your Internet provider know. Never give your password to anyone – emails from fake service providers will ask for your password. Just delete them from your mailbox without answering.

987 SAFETY FIRST

Keep a fire blanket close to the cooker to quickly muffle flames caused by fat and/or electricity – adding water to flames only makes the problem worse.

988 DAMP TEA TOWEL

Never throw water on a pan fire. Instead, turn off the heat immediately and cover with a damp tea towel or fire blanket to smother the flames.

989 ONLINE SHOPPING

Always deal with a reputable company when buying on the Internet. Check the website for their full name, postal address and phone number. Check delivery times and the refund policy; also what data the company is collecting about you. Only hand over your details if you trust the company.

990 USE A VIRUS SCANNER

Check everything sent to you with a virus scanner. Some computer viruses can steal information such as your name and address from your computer's memory. If someone you don't know sends you an email you can delete it without reading it. It is illegal to send computer viruses so if you receive an email you don't trust report it to your service provider and they will inform the police.

991 OBSCENE EMAILS

Should you receive offensive emails, don't answer them. Instead save them onto a disk before you delete them and hand it in to the police. When chatting online keep your ID a secret. Report anything obscene or threatening to your service provider. If you decide to meet anyone from a chat room or online dating agency, go to a public place where you feel safe or ask a friend along. Always let someone else know the person you plan to meet, where and when. Let them know when you're home again.

992 SCREEN CALLS

Use an answer phone to screen calls and pick up only when it's someone you want to talk to. Withhold your number when making calls to protect our privacy. Make sure your answering message doesn't reveal your name, address or phone number. If you are single, use the word 'we' in your message so callers can't tell you live alone. Ask a male friend to record your message if you are a female living alone.

993 ON THE OFFENSIVE

Just answer 'hello' when you pick up the phone so the caller doesn't have your name. Try not to say anything to an offensive or threatening caller – just replace the receiver as calmly as you can. Many callers give up if you don't reveal anything. Note down times and dates of offensive calls as evidence.

water & drains

994 WATER EVERYWHERE

Keep a good supply of old towels or rags in the house to handle washing machine, toilet, bath and sink overflows. If the worst happens, turn off the tap (faucet). Grab a bundle of old towels and use to soak up the pooling water. Use another spare towel or several smaller rags to contain the water by soaking it up from the outside toward the centre. Mop or use a wet vac. Leave to dry, using fans and dehumidifiers if necessary.

995 COPING WITH FLOODS

If flooding occurs in your home, consider the safety of you and your family first and your possessions second. Evacuate, if necessary, and call for help at a neighbour's house. Never risk electrocution by re-entering a flooded house if the electrical power is still on.

996 KNOW YOUR LOCATIONS

Take time to memorize the main shut-off for every water device in your home including sinks, toilets, water heaters, dishwashers, washing machines and dryers. Also learn the main shut-off point for the whole house.

997 BE A SLUDGE-BUSTER

If you have a slow-moving drain, sludge is building up in the pipe. Pour 100 g (3½ oz) of salt into the drain followed by 100 g (3½ oz) bicarbonate of soda. Now pour a full kettle of boiling water down the drain to break down the clog – avoid turning on the tap (faucet) for a few hours to allow the solution to really get working.

988 WATER LEAKS

If a water pipe breaks or a leak develops, call your local water company and they will turn it off at the outside valve. If the situation seems to be getting out of hand, call in professional help. Floods from drains and other plumbing problems can cause untold damage to your property and anyone living below you.

989 FROZEN PIPES

First, open the tap (faucet) that is supplied by the frozen pipe – if you don't the steam you create while heating the pipe could burst the pipe. Wrap the pipe with several layers of towelling and pour hot water over the top. Repeat several times until the pipe becomes unfrozen.

1000 SODA SIZZLER

Blocked drain? Pour 50 ml (2 fl oz) bicarbonate of soda down the kitchen sink followed by the same amount of white vinegar. See how the mixture fizzes and bubbles. Don't worry: it's harmless. Wait 30 minutes, and then flush with cool water.

1001 BLOCKED SINK

For a total blockage, place a bowl or bucket beneath the sink to catch the dirty water. Undo the U-shaped trap below and remove the blockage with a wire coat hanger.

221

INDEX

ACKNOWLEDGEMENTS

I would like to thank my editor Lisa Dyer at Carlton for giving me the opportunity to write this book and for being a true friend. Thanks also to designers Zoë Dissell and Ed Pickford for a great-looking book and to Carol Morley for her inspired illustrations. Several of my other friends were happy to share their housekeeping tips with me and to help with my research. They are: Joanne Brooks, Kim Browne, Diana Craig, Amanda Eglash, Nicky Gyopari, Clive Hebard, Lesley Levene, Caroline Sangster, my sister Julie Sexton, Miranda Stonor and Louise Turpin. With 1001 tips to find, I am most grateful to them!

I would also like to thank my personal trainer Patricia Braz (www.fitappeal.co.uk) for keeping me in good shape to write the book. Last, but definitely not least, I would like to thank Shaun Barrington for advice on asthma and Egyptian cotton; also for his constant support and encouragement. This is my first book and it is dedicated to him because I love him dearly.